Urban Revolt

Urban Revolt

State Power and the Rise of People's Movements in the Global South

Edited by Trevor Ngwane, Luke Sinwell, and Immanuel Ness

Haymarket Books
Chicago, Illinois

Published in 2017 by
Haymarket Books
P.O. Box 180165
Chicago, IL 60618
773-583-7884
www.haymarketbooks.org
info@haymarketbooks.org

ISBN: 978-1-60846-713-6

Trade distribution:
In the US, Consortium Book Sales and Distribution, www.cbsd.com
In Canada, Publishers Group Canada, www.pgcbooks.ca
In the UK, Turnaround Publisher Services, www.turnaround-uk.com
All other countries, Ingram Publisher Services International, intlsales@perseusbooks.com

This book was published with the generous support of Lannan Foundation and Wallace
Action Fund.

Cover design by Eric Ruder. Cover image of a protest in Mumbai courtesy of Bilal Khan.

Printed in Canada by union labor.

Library of Congress Cataloging-in-Publication data is available.

10 9 8 7 6 5 4 3 2 1

Contents

Part III: Urban Squatter Movements in South Asia: Kolkata and Jakarta

Introduction

Trevor Ngwane, Luke Sinwell, and Immanuel Ness

T he majority of work on urban social movements (USMs) offers theoretical perspectives and, in some cases, assumes the hegemony of the capitalist framework (see, for example, Harvey 2013). However, these studies fail to adequately interrogate the micro-processes in which the opposite is taking place: where the hegemony of ruling classes is being directly challenged by mass organizations. The sparse literature that does deal with a variety of cases across the globe offers a liberal, management-oriented perspective that does not help the reader to understand the revolutionary potential of USMs. Rather, these analyses leave us trapped within a reformist framework that will never advance the cause of global economic justice. Since major urban areas have become the principal sites of poor and working-class social upheaval in the early twenty-first century, as the arenas of the production, exchange, and reproduction of commodities, the chapters in this book explore key cities in the Global South to identify the common defining sources of USMs. Taking the case of South Africa as a lens or pivot, this book draws from cases in Asia, Latin America, and Africa more generally, further highlighting the ways in which the supremacy of multinational capital has advanced poverty, particularly in the Global South.

Through detailed case studies contributed by activists and scholars engaged in ethnographic research and participant observation, the book unravels the potential and limitations of USMs on an international level. The case studies aim to address the extent to which movements challenge not only neoliberalism but capitalism itself. How are these movements changing larger aspects of society and politics? How do individuals and organizations move beyond the boundaries of constitutional or legal constructs, and to what degree are they successful?

The methodology employed in order to construct the chapters in the book provides a unique texture, which culminates in an urgent, passionate, and persuasive chronicle of the rise of USMs. Together, they demonstrate the ways in which USMs seize control or power within the commons. In each chapter, scholars and activists at the forefront of USMs document the unfolding of this combustible process of super-exploitation, grinding poverty, state and corporate violence, and the rise of social movements rooted in the democratic aspirations of the working class of the Global South.

A central focus of each chapter is examining the lives of the individuals and social organizations who make up these modern movements confronting the state and capital. Through this dialectical study of exploitation and resistance, the significance of USMs comes to life. The reader will recognize the genuine probability that the process of resistance by mobilized working-class inhabitants seeking a voice in determining their societies is presently the most dynamic source of fundamental revolutionary social change.

South Africa as Pivotal Site for Revolutionary Change

On the slopes of a now-infamous mountain in Marikana, South Africa—just outside an operations base of the third-largest platinum mining company in the world, Lonmin—police gunned down thirty-four mineworkers on August 16, 2012. Those who had still believed that the ruling African National Congress (ANC) was a liberator of the Black masses now began to be convinced that the ANC was in fact a new oppressor.

To protect the interests of capital, the party's leaders were willing to drown independent working-class mobilization in blood. Despite the fact that the bodies of their brothers had been returned to the rural villages for burial, the vast majority of mineworkers at Lonmin intensified their strike action, employing exceptionally democratic worker committees based on the organic capacity and active consent of the rank and file. As the South African left continues to be reconfigured, with the largest trade union in the country (the National Union of Metalworkers of South Africa [NUMSA], which boasts 400,000 members) de-affiliating from the ANC, in part as a result of the massacre, it is unquestionable that the country will never be the same again.

Marikana, we believe, is symbolic of the spirit of militancy and anticapitalist struggle, which embodies a range of USMs in South Africa and offers a lens through which to understand urban revolt across the world. South Africa not only has more protests per capita than any other country in the world, it is also the most unequal country in the world. It boasts the wealthiest suburb in Africa—Sandton—and bridges the Global North/South divide, as the poor struggle to exist in informally (in some cases, illegally) occupied areas. It is no moot point that as we began to write the introduction to this book, the main contributor was in a jail, precisely for struggling with the poor for urban space and services in a community of about twenty thousand people on the outskirts of Johannesburg, which has access neither to proper sanitation nor to decent shelter (in fact, the inhabitants live in corrugated iron shacks). The crisis of capitalism has waged a war against the poor and the working class, who have been partially successful at fighting back through their own alternative governance structures and tactics such as sabotage, road blockades, unprotected strikes, and illegal electricity connections. This book makes a contribution toward understanding the rise of USMs internationally, as capitalism attempts to squeeze the working class further onto the periphery of the city spaces where the majority of the world now lives.

The Ayotzinapa Massacre: Popular Protests against Police Brutality and Social Services in Mexico

The abuse of state power and police violence in South Africa is a global phenomenon that extends to every continent. Mexico epitomizes the collusion between government, business, and law enforcement authorities in attacking innocent civilians, especially protesters seeking to restore basic services such as education, water, and housing. In Mexico, police authorities and capital are eager to resort to state violence to suppress peasant and working-class communities, in which (as is the case in South Africa) the vast majority of people are indigenous to their regions. In the Mexican case, NAFTA augured a new era of neoliberal capitalism, which has amplified inequality and expanded abject poverty. The gross distortions created under NAFTA have allowed US multinational corporations to dump agricultural products into the Mexican market, forcing peasants off the land and into the major cities of Mexico and the United States. Under NAFTA, Pemex, Mexico's state oil company, which the government is privatizing, exports unrefined petroleum to the United States for reimportation and domestic consumption. The Mexican police are now enforcing public order in an era when social services are most needed, due to the rapid growth of the country's urban population. As poverty and inequality grow and basic services and resources are removed, state and local police are resorting to violence and murder against civilians in defense of the vast expansion of drug cartels and organized crime groups.

The crisis reached a pinnacle on September 26, 2014, when students from the Ayotzinapa Normal School were attacked by police in Iguala, Guerrero, about a hundred miles due south of Mexico City. Six were shot dead. The local police then detained forty-three of the students, who disappeared—until they were found massacred, their bodies buried in many scattered sites. They had been turned over to the United Warriors organized crime group.

In the months after the students' disappearance, popular demonstrations broke out across Mexico, with millions of people demanding their return. Two months later, when public inquiries found that police had acted on orders from the mayor of Iguala to kill the students, tens of thousands of protesters converged on Mexico City to protest the Ayotzinapa killings and the murder of more than a hundred thousand other civilians from 2006 to 2014. They were met by riot police, who threw tear gas at them; they responded with rocks and Molotov cocktails. The most popular slogan among demonstrators was "Fue el estado": "The state did it." They called for the resignation of Mexican president Enrique Peña Nieto, because of his use of police force against protesters.

Like Marikana, Ayotzinapa is one of a growing number of government massacres explicitly or tacitly approved by neoliberal capitalist regimes to suppress indigenous working peoples. This book examines the emergence of USMs and mass mobilizations to demand justice and social services in such contexts. It documents similar movements happening elsewhere in the Global South among working-class people and peasants who seek to overturn neoliberalism, demanding education, housing, electricity, health care, and other social services from their governments, as well as the end of violence that is sanctioned or condoned by the state.

Chapter Goals and Objectives

Each chapter examines unique aspects of the development of unconventional communities as the predominant form of social organization in major urban areas across the world. They focus on the social organization and militancy of urban inhabitants, providing a robust historical analysis of the urban struggle in relation to at least one of three themes. The first is antiracist movements and community responses to police brutality: the hostile context within which USMs find themselves as capitalist states employ police and sometimes even the army in an attempt to stifle dissent. The next is service delivery movements, and the third is movements that seek to promote transformative methods of governance as alternatives to what is offered under the capitalist system.

The chapters focus on the role of state authorities and business (capital) in expropriating land, housing, electricity, water, and other social services in central locations, at the expense of urban communities in which the vast majority of inhabitants live in poverty. Expropriation refers to the physical dislocation of populations and the denial of essential services. The vast majority of forced evictions occur in or near major national and global cities, under the guise of economic growth and capitalist development. However, the consequences of the land evictions inure to the benefit of the upper classes and international capitalists who seek to "develop" economies for speculation through a form of rentier capitalism. Among those dispossessed of their homes are migrants whose lives exist at the margin of legality and who are crucial to the labor market, often as contract workers unregulated by the state.

Considering the speed of development and intensity of integration of global capitalist processes and the political turn to neoliberalism, which have brought about new (or refreshed) paradigms for increasing land values, productivity, and profits, each chapter of *Urban Revolt* examines the signal importance of these "invisible," precarious inhabitants who live in vulnerable conditions in communities without services: water, electricity, sanitation, and so on. Broadening research on this underworld of urban communities is important to understanding the process of capital accumulation, which is rooted in land speculation.

In examining the social organization of urban militancy, authors were also asked to respond to one or more of the following questions and themes:

- The nature of eviction, rooted in illegality, violence, and other forms of forced removal. How do poor and working-class residents resist government evictions?
- Urban militancy often results in the imposition of state violence. In what ways do urban movements respond to police brutality?
- The dominant form of government practiced by the state tends to exclude the vast majority of the urban population from participating in decision-making processes that affect their lives. Is it possible to decipher an alternative form of governance, which is practiced by urban movements?
- In what ways does the form of social organization and militancy change larger aspects of society and politics, including capitalist development?
- Geographical research is concentrated on struggles over land and resources at the community and neighborhood levels. What is unique and what is universal in your case study? What insights into daily life,

organization, and resistance among marginalized urban workers can be applied to other cases?

- How do the economic environments, regulatory regimes, and government policies influence the forms of struggle and repression?
- How do individuals and organizations attempt to move beyond the boundaries of constitutional or legal constructs, and to what degree are they successful?
- What lessons can be learned from the case study in your chapter?

Part I: African Movements of the Urban Poor

Part one draws from case studies on the African continent and begins with two chapters from South Africa, one on urban slum dwellers in a squatter settlement southwest of Johannesburg and another on Marikana, the site of the uprising of mineworkers in the platinum mining belt north of Johannesburg. The third chapter in this section examines the rise of a militant urban-slum-dweller movement in Lagos, Nigeria, resisting gentrification and displacement.

Chapter 1, titled "Thembelihle Burning, Hope Rising," by Luke Sinwell, examines the community movement of slum dwellers in Johannesburg in a context where workers and the poor have come to the realization that the time for Mandela mania has long ended. Poverty has persisted since the end of apartheid. Moreover, South Africa is now arguably the protest capital of the world. Sinwell's chapter investigates the political forms that have been sustained for more than a decade in one of the most militant communities in the country. The community is called Thembelihle, an informal settlement to the southwest of Johannesburg made up of approximately twenty thousand people. Sinwell focuses specifically on a socialist organization called the Thembelihle Crisis Committee (TCC), which was formed in 2001 and 2002 as a response to the municipality's attempts to evict people from the area. Though the community had experienced major protests throughout the 2000s and early 2010s, 2015 witnessed its most potent upsurge, involving road blockages and other demonstrations and lasting more than three weeks. The chapter offers an ethnographic description of the origins and historical development of this specific protest, which resulted in a major state concession when the provincial government announced that the area would be formalized and electrified, something that many residents had only dreamed of before. It concludes by exploring the possibilities for the TCC and its community to play a leading role in the political moment in which South Africa finds itself after Marikana.

In chapter 2, "Against All Odds: The 'Spirit of Marikana' and the Resurgence of the Working-Class Movement in South Africa," Trevor Ngwane examines the rise of a militant workers' movement twenty years after the fall of apartheid and how the Marikana massacre of August 16, 2012, was a signal turning point in the South African workers' movement. Ngwane links his historical work on self-government in an informal settlement, Nkaneng (which is in Marikana), to the specific case of workers mobilizing at the Lonmin platinum mine. The paper contextualizes the case within the broader landscape and demographics related to the mushrooming of shacks in the Rustenburg "platinum city."

Ngwane asserts that the strike was expressive of the organic capacity of the working class: that is, the ability of workers to drive history forward and to lead the struggle for human emancipation. This capacity was demonstrated during the anti-apartheid struggle and largely suppressed and denied in the twenty years of post-apartheid freedom; the latter period has been characterized by a concerted neoliberal onslaught on working-class rights and living standards. However, the phenomenal increase in disruptive street protests in working-class communities since 2004 and the two massive public sector strikes of 2007 and 2010 were signs that this fighting capacity and historical agency were still alive. Marikana emphatically signaled this, and its aftermath—namely, the five-month-long strike by platinum miners in 2014 and the decision of NUMSA, the biggest trade union in South Africa, to break out of the Tripartite Alliance between the ANC, the South African Communist Party (SACP) and the Congress of South African Trade Unions (COSATU), arguably the cornerstone of the architecture of class collaboration—suggests a new dawn and new vigor in the workers' movement in the country. This union's immediate political project is to build a united front of labor, community, and youth organizations and movements in struggle against neoliberalism, and its aim in the longer term is to spearhead a movement for socialism and form a workers' party.

Ngwane explores these developments from a historical sociological perspective through critically examining current scholarly approaches to social movement studies, and he suggests that some analyses do not fully appreciate the underlying socio-historical dynamics. Scholar activists require research agendas and theories that facilitate rather than retard our understanding of the processes involved in the rebuilding of the working-class movement in this country and in the world. Toward this end we need to support the quest for the development of a Marxist theory of social movements.

Chapter 3, by Ayokunle Omobowale, "Makoko Slum Settlement: Migrant Peasants on the Lagos Lagoon, Nigeria," explores popular resistance against gentrification within sub-Saharan Africa's most populous city. With an estimated population of 200,000, Lagoon Makoko exists as a major habitation for migrant peasants who have constructed comfort and prosperity out of the precarious conditions of the slum. Makoko has existed for over a century, and it has survived repeated official demolition attempts. This research was carried out with the aid of both quantitative and qualitative methods to probe the context of migration, the social organization of stilt housing, and the challenges and survival strategies of Makoko settlers. The study discovered that people are chain-migrated by family and friends to Lagoon Makoko due to its vibrant peasant economic landscape, which allows huge financial gains to settlers. Makoko's stilt housing presents an intricate property system of inheritance, tenancy, and sale involving "landlords," property agents, tenants, and stilt artisans who are constantly in economic exchange relationships. Makoko challenges are tackled through periodic environmental sanitation and public advocacy against demolition.

Part II: Protest and Struggle in Latin America

In Part II, we examine the rise and expansion of a broad repertoire of resistance to police repression and economic dislocation in Latin America, site of many of the world's major slums and impoverished communities. In chapter 4, "The Ayotzinapa Massacre: Mexico's Popular Protests and New Landscapes of Indignation," Claudia Delgado Villegas examines the urban protests in Mexico City and throughout Mexico in the wake of the Ayotzinapa massacre that occurred in Iguala, Guerrero, in Mexico on September 26, 2014, within the broad context of the current governance and social crisis in Mexico after three decades of NAFTA and the latest wave of neoliberal labor and economic reforms. The chapter illuminates, on the one hand, the current forms of social organization and militancy shown on the streets, and on the other the deep historic and spatial connections rooted in long-term class struggle and resistance in Mexico.

From the autumn of 2014 to the spring of 2015, Mexico City experienced the awakening of popular protests, with millions of demonstrators marching to the Zócalo—the country's major public square—to demand justice for Ayotzinapa. The chapter analyzes the awakening of this urban revolt in the city as it generates a complex landscape of contestation in which the protests for Ayotzinapa are at the same time reviving a long-term dispute for the use of public space in the city, within the context of expanding urban neoliberalism.

Rather than being conclusive, the chapter looks to the Ayotzinapa massacre as a lens through which to reflect on the connection between contemporary social movements and the city, to illuminate the city as an arena of class struggle and a contemporary landscape of contestation all over the world. The research is based on qualitative methodologies combining ethnography, visual records, documents, and fieldwork conducted in Mexico City from 2013 to 2015.

Over the last thirty years, Brazil has witnessed a tumultuous variety of social movements: LGBT, antiracist, feminist, and many others. Nevertheless, a dictatorship that lasted more than two decades (1964–1985) settled its coercive apparatus in Rio de Janeiro, Brazil's capital until 1960. Chapter 5, "The Case of the West Zone: Urban Revolt and Social Movement Adaptations in Rio de Janeiro, Brazil," by Simone da Silva Ribeiro Gomes, discusses the highly coercive environment for social movements in Rio de Janeiro's West Zone, especially in the neighborhoods of Realengo, Campo Grande, and Santa Cruz. Like many Latin American urban spaces, those areas must deal with multiple violent actors, such as drug-trafficking gangs, an extremely violent police force, and militias that control economic activity and impose a strong moral code, threatening to kill inhabitants who don't follow their rules. This being the case, the possibilities for social action are severely restricted. Based on a qualitative methodology, with an ethnographic inspiration and semistructured interviews of young militants in distinct social movements who were born and raised in those peripheries, this chapter aims to trace some common patterns in the ways popular movements manage to establish themselves in different contexts with violent actors. The strategies the militants developed in those urban settlements had to take on state violence, fighting militias, and police repression in distinct and performative ways, moving toward cultural and educational solutions in order to more freely discuss the problems they faced on a daily basis while avoiding any resemblance to an urban revolt, which would draw police attention to them.

Chapter 6, by Patrick O'Hare—"The Uruguayan Recyclers' Union: *Clasificadores*, Circulation, and the Challenge of Mobile Labor Organization"— focuses on the importance of circulation to the organizing of Uruguayan waste pickers and informal-sector labor more generally. Research is based on ethnographic fieldwork conducted in 2009–10 and 2014–15 with the Uruguayan *clasificador* trade union, the Unión de Clasificadores de Residuos Urbanos Sólidos (UCRUS). *Clasificadores* is the name given in Uruguay to workers dedicated to recovering recyclable materials, principally cardboard, paper, plastics, and metal. They work in the streets with a bicycle and cart or horse and cart; at the municipal landfill; or in cooperatives and at municipal plants. There are estimated to be between three and nine thousand clasificadores in Montevideo alone, and the group is widely considered to be the most exploited link in the national recycling chain. Their low incomes, lack of social security, and exposure to environmental risk are seen as subsidizing the profits of the formal recycling sector (Elizalde et al., 2012). Given these circumstances, Patrick O'Hare sets out to explore the distinguishing features of trade union organizing within the Uruguayan informal recycling sector. In the absence of key traditional union tactics such as striking, how did the UCRUS attempt to pressure or leverage its antagonists? How did it attempt to organize such a dispersed sector, and which of its constituency's issues did it have to mediate?

Part III: Urban Squatter Movements in South Asia: Kolkata and Jakarta

The next two chapters explore cities in Asia.

Chapter 7, by Swapna Banerjee-Guha, "The Nonadanga Eviction in Kolkata: Contemporary Urban Development and People's Resistance," explores neoliberal concepts of place marketing, infrastructural efficiency, and competitiveness that have become emblematic of Indian cities in the twenty-first century. Urban reform in India, deeply entrenched in the priorities of the market, has been characterized by privatization of urban development, increasing involvement of international institutions in reform prescriptions, and persistent dispossession of the poor. To appease big capital, urban planning in India has freed itself from obsolete ideas of planning for the majority and busied itself with making "smarter," more investment-friendly cities.

With a shrunken organized sector and nonexpandable employment base, the cities are no longer centers for permanent jobs or alternative economic bases for the poorer migrants who continue to flock to them, driven to desperation by a thoroughly stagnant rural sector. Indian cities under the neoliberal order hence concentrate not only a disproportionate share of capital but also a large number of the disadvantaged and thereby emerge as prospective spaces of conflict and resistance. Increasing segregation of the city space and problems with regulatory access to work and resources link the issue of the "right to the city" to that of the "right to livelihood," lending contemporary USMs a distinct class content. The chapter proposes that this new politics of claims will go a long way toward defining the future of neoliberal urbanism in India and will pave ways for launching new class struggles as well as struggles for citizenship rights.

Chapter 8, "The Struggle of the Urban Poor against Forced Eviction in Jakarta," by Muhammad Ridha, focuses on the ways in which forced eviction in Jakarta is inseparable from the development of contemporary cities. Each year, hundreds of thousands of urban dwellers are displaced from their livelihoods in cities around the world. As the number of people living in poverty has risen from 17% to 28% over the last ten years, forced eviction has seemed to offer a way of taking more control over urban development, clearing the way for the construction of infrastructure (lights, roads, sewage) and services (health care, education). Optimistic as it is, this view neglects the real process of the city itself. The current form of urban process, a policy of slum clearance and urban development aimed solely at economic growth, has created a discriminatory city and could potentially lead to its own destruction. Yet the rampant poverty to which forced eviction is a (misguided) response can also be a fertile ground for the emergence of reactionary consciousness among the urban poor.

Conclusion

As Davis's (2006) essential work highlighted a decade ago, the urban poor and working class make up the majority of the world's population, and this segment continues to grow—not only in the South but increasingly in parts of the North as well. The purpose of this book was to map and analyze the ways in which the majority of the world exists and struggles in the contemporary urban context and to unpack the ways in which this has challenged or transformed how the city is organized. On a national level, we think here of the "Rebellion of the Poor" project currently being undertaken by the South African Research Chair in Social Change at the University of Johannesburg (Alexander 2010). The project is the most extensive, and possibly the most important, investigation into the nature of popular resistance in poor areas in post-apartheid South Africa. The process of compiling this book has enabled us to develop a network of scholars and activists researching and organizing in various cities in the Global South. The research we envision undertaking over the next several years will of course describe, analyze, and develop theory, but it also has a practical objective. It is based on the tenet that no revolution can be victorious in one corner of the world. Nor is gaining access to "the right to the city," as David Harvey forcefully argued, "an end in itself" (Harvey 2013, xviii). For the editors, this book is the beginning of a much more thorough political research project that aims to link isolated struggles in urban areas more integrally to each other on both a national and international scale.

Part I:
African Movements
of the Urban Poor

Chapter 1

Thembelihle Burning, Hope Rising

Luke Sinwell

> *I tell our people that the workers of Marikana did not get anything until they stood up and fought, sacrificed, for what was rightfully theirs. We [in Thembelihle] must continue to bring this spirit [of Marikana] to our own doorstep and into the streets. If we sit quietly and patiently, the capitalists will win and we will remain defeated.*
> **—Hendrick More, Thembelihle resident, March 15, 2015**

Themba lay restless in his neighbor's shack throughout the night and into the early hours of the morning during the major protest that lasted for three weeks during February and March of 2015. Each sound that he heard signaled, from his perspective, the approach of police officers who had come to arrest him. Themba's informal settlement, Thembelihle (a Zulu word meaning "good hope"), twenty-five miles from Johannesburg, South Africa, was witnessing an unofficial state of emergency. It had become, in recent weeks, a hot spot of resistance, which included the particularly effective tactic of road blockages. These were designed to attract attention from the government, since they prevented those in the neighboring middle-class Indian suburb of Lenasia from going about their daily business. The police had identified leaders of the Thembelihle Crisis Committee (TCC), an overtly socialist community organization representing a large portion of the settlement's nearly twenty thousand residents, for their key role in coordinating demonstrations in the area. Their pictures, including Themba's, had been placed on the walls of the Lenasia police station where dozens of other residents were still detained.

Johannesburg, the economic hub of South Africa, aspires to become "a world-class African city," but residents of Thembelihle, who live in its poorest region (region G), have little to celebrate more than twenty years into democracy (Murray 2008; Tomlinson et al., 2003). History has demonstrated that the only time the triple burden of poverty, unemployment, and inequality has been eased, with residents gaining minor concessions from the state in the form of basic service delivery, is when organized formations have entered the streets in large numbers, relentlessly and over extended periods of time. In my own reading, TCC has been the most militant explicitly socialist community-based organization in the post-apartheid period. Its mottos are anticapitalist, its own ideals and practices challenge some of the key tenets of the capitalist system, and its leaders, as well as many rank-and-file members of the organization, exhibit a culture of defiance. It can be said with confidence that Thembelihle, like Marikana, is a jewel in the crown of those who seek to build an anticapitalist alternative.

Daniel Bovu, who had formerly been the local government councilor of the ward in which Thembelihle is located, failed to deliver any houses during his tenure as an African National Congress (ANC) leader, which began with the first local government elections in 1999. The dire material conditions in Thembelihle signified to residents that their home was indeed a microcosm of failed service delivery for the country as a whole, which had been witnessing increasing inequality and poverty since the first democratic elections of 1994 (Saul and Bond 2014; Bond 2000). In 1996, the ANC adopted the neoliberal Growth Employment and Redistribution (GEAR) policy, creating the conditions in which local service delivery was not a priority: rather, the so-called welfare state would be rolled back, and the free market and foreign direct investment would prevail. Though the ANC had played an undeniably courageous and heroic role in the struggle for Black liberation in the face of the racist and repressive apartheid regime throughout much of the twentieth century, the "Mandela Rainbow Nation" had become in the post-apartheid period but a figment of the imagination of international anti-apartheid activists, as well as of those inside the country who had, among other reasons perhaps, either been enticed by the token welfare system of the ANC or sought to maintain the status quo in order to preserve their own interests. New social movements, with "new" meaning "formed in the post-apartheid period," emerged in the late 1990s and early 2000s in this context (Ballard, Habib, and Valodia 2006).

As had become a prevalent, if not predominant, practice inside the ANC, leaders of the party benefited from the despondency of the masses and were even encouraged not to deliver services to people living in poor communities. Bovu was thus paradoxically promoted to Member of the Mayoral Committee (MMC) of Local Government of Human Settlements in the much larger Gauteng region despite his failure to deliver to one of the most impoverished areas in Johannesburg. He had become, in a word, the archenemy of many of the residents of Thembelihle, one with whom the TCC was nevertheless willing to engage, on its own terms, in order to achieve one of its primary objectives: obtaining service delivery.

By mid-2014, after more than twelve years of engaging local government officials around questions of service delivery, TCC leaders made a strategic decision to escalate issues from the local government to the provincial, taking their case to Gauteng officials (Gauteng is one of South Africa's nine provinces). They decided to target the Gauteng Member of the Executive Committee (MEC) for Housing, Jacob Mamabolo. In November of that year, representatives of the TCC engaged the MEC's office around the issue of the upgrading of the community. Previously, Thembelihle had been declared an unsafe area in which to develop housing settlements due to the claim that the area was dolomitic (though residents argued otherwise). Now, after sustained pressure from the community over more than a decade, officials were willing to negotiate. Thembelihle was to be declared a formal area and earmarked for development.

At a meeting in mid-December 2014, held between representatives of the MEC and the leaders of the TCC, authorities promised that they would respond to residents' demands, requesting that they be given the full month of January 2015 to get a plan in place. By February, the TCC had heard nothing. Upon their report back to the community on February 21, 2015, and in the midst of an attempt by the TCC to put an end to the attacks and theft that were taking place on foreigners' small shops in the informal settlement, a decision was made to embark on action in the streets the next morning, starting at 4:00 a.m. No one was to go to work. Those attempting to pass the area would be stopped, and their cars would be smashed if those occupying the streets deemed it necessary.

This move culminated in a three-week-long road blockage and strike and an unofficial state of emergency in the settlement, with seventy-five residents arrested, three hospitalized, and one murdered. It would ultimately lead to an official decision to formalize the settlement, thus making it legal and setting the stage for the delivery of basic services such as water, electricity, and housing, which the community had been fighting for even prior to the dawn of the democratic dispensation of 1994. Earlier critiques of South African organizations like the TCC have tended to highlight the local nature of grassroots mobilization and the ability of the state's ruling party to intervene with minor concessions and thereby co-opt a movement (Sinwell 2011; Dawson and Sinwell 2012). The TCC, however, has been able to avoid this pitfall, due in large part to its broad socialist outlook and firm commitment to the working class on a national and even international level.

Drawing from earlier scholarly work and the available documents, I will first provide some background on the politics of the TCC and some details relating to the establishment of the informal settlement in which the organization is located. Thereafter, I will rely on my own participant observation inside the movement as well as interviews with leading members of the community in order to capture the intimate details of the events that took place in 2014 and 2015. To conclude, I will explore the potential of the TCC to contribute to the achievement of a socialist alternative in South Africa and beyond.

Background

The informal settlement called Thembelihle is part of Lenasia, which is located in a predominantly Indian suburb southwest of the city of Johannesburg. Thembelihle has been growing since the late 1980s and early 1990s, when people first occupied the area. People were reportedly told by the ANC (which, prior to coming into power, was one of the most militant organizations in the country) to "take what belongs to you!" (Le Roux 2014, 119) The settlement is now the home of approximately sixteen or seventeen thousand people, almost all designated Black, who live in seven or eight thousand shacks (Pingo 2013, 14; Le Roux 2014, 117).

When the ANC won the first nonracial elections in 1994, Thembelihle remained state-owned land. Nelson Mandela himself visited the settlement and "promised a better life and secured tenure" (Le Roux 2014, 119). During the "honeymoon" period in post-apartheid South Africa, from 1994 until the late 1990s, residents had reason to be optimistic. It seemed that the ANC, under the state-centered and people-driven Reconstruction and Development Programme (RDP), would deliver for the previously disadvantaged: for those who had been oppressed under the apartheid regime. But to a large extent this did not happen. In mid-2002, in fact, the state attempted to evict the people of Thembelihle on the grounds that they were on unsafe dolomitic land prone to catastrophic sinkholes (the TCC argues that this is not necessarily the case). They sent in the Red

Ants security company (who carry guns and "sting" when people refuse to move) to enforce the eviction order. According to Segodi:

> They wanted to move us without proper consultation. Unlike in the previous regime where the state could just remove people from one place to another, now one needs to have a court order if they are to forcefully remove people from land. And that process was not followed. Well, there were talks of people who wanted to move to Vlakfontein, but on that day, they did not identify those people. They just came and demolished any shack that they came across, and that to us constituted forced removal, because they were even taking shacks of people who were not on the list of those who wanted to move. So they wanted to use the so-called consent of the minority to remove everyone from Thembelihle. (Le Roux 2014, 122)

The TCC, which was established in 2001 when the city of Johannesburg announced its plan to relocate the community, successfully organized against the evictions in 2002. In the eyes of many residents, the organization had become a legitimate representative of the people, capable of fighting alongside them.

Throughout the 2000s, the TCC continued to hold weekly mass meetings and elect its executives at annual meetings. They made countless attempts at engaging local government and used other tactics such as illegally connecting electricity from the neighboring suburbs and installing their own pipes for water in order to bring services directly to the community. Nearly every family in Thembelihle now has access to running water and electricity. In 2011, about a decade after the TCC had been established, the community held a major demonstration in the area, which was, according to Le Roux, "the biggest protest thus far from the Thembelihle community" (2014, 129). As they had done on many other occasions, they submitted a memorandum to local officials, but when the officials did not respond within the period stipulated, the TCC reported back to the community to put their destiny in their own hands. On the one hand, the TCC is a socialist organization whose constitution states that its objective is to "advance our struggles against capitalist deprivation guided by the vision of socialism" (see Le Roux 2014, 147). On the other, the hallmark political orientation of the TCC is that as a radically democratic organizational culture it takes its lead from the community, thereby facilitating popular participation from below. One coordinator put it succinctly: "We are not a militant organization; we just do what the community wants."

The TCC is not alone. It had reached out to a wide range of political currents, from the Anti-Privatisation Forum (APF—a powerful anticapitalist civic umbrella in the early to mid-2000s, which has since waned) to the Democratic Left Front (DLF—formalized in 2011 as an anticapitalist alternative to the ANC). It has also joined the Marikana Support Campaign (MSC), Black Lives Matter, and campaigns against police brutality in other parts of southern Africa, such as Zimbabwe. The TCC in conjunction with the nearby Soweto Electricity Crisis Committee (SECC) forms part of a socialist electoral front called the Operation Khanyisa Movement (OKM).

The OKM is directly accountable to the two civic organizations, and the one councilor who has a seat in the city of Johannesburg has signed a pledge stipulating that 100% of her salary will go to the organization (OKM) and that she will be paid a living wage. The councilor resides in Thembelihle and is organically linked to struggles inside Thembelihle and Soweto as well as to struggles that take place in the rest of the country, both among workers and within communities. The SECC, TCC, and OKM each contribute to international solidarity efforts on a regular basis, most recently in a demonstration at the US embassy in Sandton against incidents of police brutality that had occured in the United States.

It is clear that the TCC is now by far the most notable organization representing the community in the area. For example, in Le Roux's (2014, 118) postgraduate survey she found that "42% of respondents said they had attended TCC meetings (either mass meetings or weekly general meetings) in 2013, in comparison to 23% who had attended ANC meetings during the same time." The next section discusses the organization's most recent (and arguably its most politicized and powerful) mobilization, which took place in 2015. The negotiations that took place between the TCC and government officials in 2014 and 2015, when the road barricade lasting three weeks took place, will be discussed in the following section.

Temperature Rising

Mass action by any community, in this case Thembelihle, never happens in a vacuum and therefore must be understood in its distinct historical context. The community, all the time living in impoverished conditions, had in fact shown patience as well as perseverance. Not only had the TCC been consistently engaging local government for more than a decade since its inception in 2001, it had, in consultation with the community in 2014 (prior to undertaking the road occupation of 2015, which is the subject of the next section), decided to elevate its demands to the provincial administration. As the organization's secretary, Siphiwe Segodi, explained when I interviewed him in June 2015:

All along we have been trying to engage with local government. And sometime in the middle of last year [2014], we concluded that we are constantly hitting the wall here, nothing is coming forth from the local government. Sometimes undertakings are made [by officials], but there's nothing, we've seen no action afterwards. . . . [In] 2014 we came to the conclusion that, no, let's abandon our engagement with local government and elevate our matter to a higher authority, which is, we identified the Department of [what is] now called Human Settlement from Housing as our primary target.

They sought to engage directly with MEC Mamabolo, who represented this department. The call for him to address the community would become a key feature of the struggle in the months to follow. A leader of the community by the name of Bhayzer, who was a member of the TCC, hand-delivered a memorandum to Mamabolo's office in mid-2014. They then obtained a signed and stamped letter from the department acknowledging the TCC's request to meet with the MEC.

By October, however, the MEC had made no effort to meet with the community representatives. The TCC (as always, in consultation with the community) decided that "we need[ed] to take a further step, and a further step was that we need[ed] to march to the office of the MEC now. . . . We need[ed] some kind of mass mobilization to put weight to our call" (Segodi interview). There was some discussion as to whether the residents would be able to obtain transport in order to march to the provincial offices of the MEC, which were located twenty-five miles away in the center of Johannesburg. It was decided that because the TCC lacked the necessary resources to have a large march in Johannesburg, residents would instead demonstrate at the municipal offices within walking distance, a mere half-mile from Thembelihle. The target of the MEC would nevertheless remain the same despite the destination. Two thousand people marched to the municipal offices on October 16. According to one resident: "People have been marching for ages and nothing is coming . . . [so] we celebrated that kind of turnout as a success" (Segodi interview). An official was sent from the MEC's office in place of Mamabolo to meet the residents and receive the memorandum, which was handed over and signed. It gave the MEC seven days to respond to the residents.

Siphiwe Segodi was appointed by the community as an official liason, mandated to follow up by email. Before the end of the seven days a representative from the MMC, Vulindlela Magebula, responded to confirm the receipt of the memorandum and further request that they be given an extension. However, the TCC refused to grant one on the basis that this was a delay tactic:

So together with the community, we agreed that you know, these kind of responses we are used to them, it has become the modus operandi of . . . state functionaries or government institutions, to say, you know, "we need more time," and then you give them more time, nothing still comes forth, so, [we] responded in line with the community's response, that this response is unacceptable and [in reality] it's a nonresponse because we were expecting that within seven days you'll be telling us what you'll be doing with the issues that we have raised. . . . We as TCC said, "We can't take this issue further. We want you guys to come down and make that pronouncement directly to the community. We want [the] MEC [Mamabolo] himself to come and make that pronouncement to the community." (Segodi interview)

In an attempt to prevent further action, Mamabolo went to Thembelihle at the end of October to address a mass meeting of the community. The MEC promised a further meeting with community representatives, which was held the following week, on November 4, 2014. A number of promises were made by senior officials regarding issues of service delivery inside and outside of Thembelihle. Mamabolo agreed to report back to the community in December (before the holidays, when South Africans tend to take a break from work and spend time with their families), but he failed to do so. The TCC decided to give him the benefit of the doubt and continued to delay any further action. When January 2015 came, the residents of Thembelihle continued to show patience with the fact that the MEC had broken his promises: "We opened as TCC, sat our [biweekly] meetings. And then . . . the time is moving but nothing . . . is coming forth. But it's January. Maybe they are still putting their things together into place. Let's see what will happen in February. We gave them another grace [period] in January" (Segodi interview).

However, when mid-February came, a number of residents including leaders of the TCC started saying to each other, "No. Now we can't allow things to move beyond this. What are we doing, comrades? No, we need action." It was agreed that the matter needed to be elevated to the mass meeting in order "to engage the community—to say, you know, all those promises that we came [back to the mass meeting] to report on here, don't seem to be materializing" (Segodi interview).

A mass meeting was held on Sunday, February 22. The TCC reported back to the community about the officials' apparent delay tactics and offered them a platform to express themselves. Members of the TCC prompted the community in radically democratic tradition to take their destiny into their own hands. "What is the next step? What should we do now?" those who called the meeting asked. A resident of the community whom I interviewed in June 2015—he preferred to remain anonymous, but I mentioned him at the beginning of this chapter under the name "Themba"—said that community residents then reminded the TCC leaders of what an official had said late in the previous year: give them time, and "if they [the officials] don't work with us [the community] or they don't respond correctly, then we can go to the streets." The majority of residents concluded: "We can't wait any longer, these people are playing with us, are playing games now." It became clear that protest action would take place until the appropriate officials responded to the community's demands.

This demonstration, however, was not to be registered with the police. Its militancy would be defined by the community's desperation. Its objective would be to disrupt business as usual in the area around Thembelihle: the middle-class suburb of Lenasia. Road blockades in particular would prevent people from going to work and even school, thus creating a crisis and attracting media attention. From the perspective of the state, it would be an illegal protest, which would require heavy police intervention. The question now was when the protest would start. Some residents argued that as soon as the mass meeting ended that afternoon, they must begin. The majority concluded that people should wake up early in the morning, in the darkness, on the following day, gather numbers, and then occupy the streets. According to Themba, "That was a decision that was made by the community, and then we as [the] TCC have to do what the community tells us to do."

Thembelihle Burning

After the mass meeting, the TCC held its own caucus to discuss how to operationalize the community's decision. Themba was tasked, along with a small delegation, to collect residents who would then enter the streets. He remembered the events clearly: "We agree that tomorrow morning [February 23] we must wake up, let's meet there by the grounds, next to my house. So we went to sleep. In the morning, I didn't set an alarm; in fact, I normally wake up around 4:00 a.m. every time. So what happened is that I heard the whistles that it's time for us to wake up, I wake up, I found like four comrades."

Thembelihle is divided into different sections: D1, D2, F, and N. The delegation swelled as it passed each section, blowing whistles and knocking on the doors of people's shacks to call them to action. The numbers grew from twenty to thirty and then sixty. By the time they reached the main road they were a group of one hundred. There they met others, who had also been gathering the masses. Following the relatively controlled demonstration held the previous year and the failure of officials to respond to their demands, the community was now resorting to militancy. They barricaded the roads:

> We started singing there, burning tires, putting stones on the road, you know, big rocks, anything you can find, you know? Put [it] on the road, burn [it]. And then obviously some cars were stoned there, I mean when they tried to pass. Until the police came and then they started to patrol the traffic on our side, like the cars had to pass [on] this [other] side. Then we keep on protesting until the early hours. Where the police came and just [told] us to move. And they were shooting [rubber bullets], you know? . . . They'd throw tear gas and stuff. And [stun] grenades. Throughout the day. ("Themba" interview)

Some of the residents, particularly young men, congregated behind large sheets of corrugated metal and threw stones at the police officers who were firing rubber bullets at them. The temperature in Thembelihle had risen; now it was burning.

A man of Indian descent who lived in the surrounding middle-class area joined the police action late in the evening, around 10:00 p.m. He told the protesters that they had to move out of the area and stop the demonstration. Members of the TCC responded that they could not end the protest themselves since it was the community that had decided to initiate it.

The first day of major protest action had passed. Themba slept for a brief period and woke up Tuesday morning, on the second day of the protest, to a new situation: "Hey! There are a lot of police now. We couldn't even go to the streets . . . but we managed to go to the traffic signals [on the edge of the major road] and sing there." The unofficial siege by the state, in the form of armed police action, had now begun. The state would now employ the carrot-and-stick strategy, using negotiating processes and promises of service delivery alongside the iron fist of police presence.

That morning, the TCC was told that they would meet with a representative from the government. They deliberated over a way forward, given that an undeclared state of emergency was developing. Mamabolo, for whom the community was waiting, did not show up, but other government officials present asked the TCC to tell the community (at a mass meeting) that they would meet with them in two weeks' time. The TCC then indicated that it could not "make a decision now. You have made promises, so you can come and tell the community yourself what Mamabolo is saying" ("Themba" interview). The officials refused to address the mass meeting, presumably because they feared that they would be scolded for their lack of responsiveness or, worse, that there could be violence. The TCC concluded that the protest was now the government's responsibility, since they were refusing to speak to the community. The TCC reported back to the community at SA block, where mass meetings were normally held.

The following morning, Thursday, February 26, the man of Indian descent who had asked members of the community to end the protest unleashed a gun. Instead of shooting rubber bullets to stun, as the police had, he sprayed live ammunition at a group of protesters. Three people were wounded and sent to a nearby hospital; another young man was killed. The media was now present and the police were attempting to negotiate with the protesters. However, the protesters were reluctant to engage in negotiation: it seemed too dangerous. They thought it likely at this stage that if they met with the police, they would be arrested:

> Now I think it is time for us to move a little bit back . . . they are going to shoot now. Because they were wearing these vests and stuff. They would take out guns. We said, "No, let's take the comrades to [our mass meeting point] Park Station." I think it was around 11:00 a.m. We went to Park Station; we had a meeting there. And then we agreed that, no, I think we need to send a delegation to talk to the commissioner or the police [officer] who is in charge there. To tell [the police] that that they don't have to shoot people; people are protesting peacefully. ("Themba" interview)

The delegation consisted of fifty to sixty people, including activist Trevor Ngwane, who had throughout the TCC's existence played a key role in shaping the organization's politics, providing solidarity and injecting a socialist ideology. Having heard about the ongoing violence in the area, he went to find out what was happening on the ground and to offer his negotiation skills. The delegation raised their hands up as if to say "don't shoot" and to offer a sign of peace. They sang the hymn "Senzenina?"—"What Have We Done?" ("Themba" interview). The majority sat down, and three people, including Trevor, went directly to the commissioner to request that the police refrain from shooting at the residents. They argued that it was their right to protest.

The police did not heed their request and instead proceeded to arrest fifteen of the people who had been seated. When Trevor asked why they were arresting them, the police responded by arresting him and another activist as well. A total of thirty-six people were arrested, and some days later a further thirty-six were arrested. According to the secretary of the TCC, who escaped arrest and has substantial legal experience surrounding the freedom of expression and the right to protest: "All the arrests were unprovoked and not justifiable in terms of the law. The first group were arrested when they peacefully sought a meeting with the police commanders" (Segodi 2015). The struggle had intensified to a point where meetings of half a dozen people were no longer tolerated by police officials, and an unofficial state of emergency was now in place in the area.

As the demonstrations continued to wax and wane in the midst of the ongoing siege, promises were made to the community that the MEC would arrive, but he did not do so. The Gauteng provincial government, in the meantime, accused community leaders of abusing platforms for engagement. On March 17, 2015—three weeks since the start of the protest—intimidation, arrests, and detentions continued in the area, and one man was shot at point-blank range by the police with rubber bullets. One resident who witnessed the shooting thought the man being fired on might not survive; fortunately, he did.

Solidarity actions from a range of organizations (including TCC's sister in struggle, the SECC, and an NGO called the Right to Know Campaign (R2K) as well as umbrella social movements like the DLF) intervened in the area. Bail funds were created to support and release those arrested. Most importantly, the residents of Thembelihle had not given up. In addition, they now had external support from sympathetic and progressive forces. The tides were shifting.

The United Front (UF), which was formed by the National Union of Metalworkers of South Africa (NUMSA), the largest trade union in South Africa, became involved as well. The UF is currently in an embryonic stage, seeking to unite workplace, community, and student struggles in the country. One of the main reasons that prompted NUMSA to form the UF was the Marikana massacre, which they viewed as resulting from the ANC's attempt to quell working-class power in the platinum belt (see Trevor Ngwane's chapter in this volume). After the police occupied Thembelihle, the UF, alongside the organizations listed above, sought to intervene before the state caused severe damage yet again. The UF called for "concrete and active solidarity with the people of Thembelihle. We call on all to join tomorrow's Mass Solidarity Meeting (1st April 2015) to end the siege in Thembelihle which will be held from 5:00 p.m. at the Park Station" (United Front Press Statement, 2015).

As one leader of the UF stated in a similar context, "if you are on your own, the capitalist class will divide, crush, and even kill you. The struggle must not be isolated. You must gather as wide a base as possible in order to confront the enemy" (pers. comm. with UF activist, January 16, 2016). The meeting was a success; the protest receded. Some leaders of the TCC believe that their victory might not have been possible had it not been for this and other interventions of outside progressive forces.

Hope Rising

"Gauteng Provincial Government and the City of Johannesburg have assured the people of Thembelihle today that the provision of basic services such as water and electricity will be accelerated as a response to pressing issues in the community."

—Gauteng Province, 2015

While many activists had consistently been involved in organizing demonstrations in the area, others had often told leaders of the TCC, including Siphiwe Mbatha (who later related his experiences to me), that these protests were getting nowhere—thus suggesting that the community was trapped in a perpetual state of informality and perhaps even despair. But that despair has been countered by both hope and practical improvements in the lives of residents. On April 24, 2015, a historic meeting took place between MEC Jacob Mamabolo, Daniel Bovu (the city of Johannesburg MMC for Housing), and the TCC. When viewed out of its historical context, the accelerated response by these government officials to "pressing issues in the community" may appear simply as part of the city's ongoing plan to improve poor people's lives. As this chapter has demonstrated, however, this is an inadequate explanation.

The improved delivery of services in Thembelihle is the result of sustained pressure from the community as well as the ability of the TCC itself to harness the community's power over more than a decade—despite the imminent threat of police brutality and repression. As the electricity poles are finally being built in late 2015, it is clear that change is possible when people use extra-institutional means to achieve their objectives. Transformation and objective improvements become evident when organizations are formed and sustained over long periods of time through the discipline of mass meetings as well as regular weekly meetings.

It also clear to the most experienced activists in places like Thembelihle that there is a much wider struggle going on. The key question for the UF, and indeed for any umbrella movement that seeks to build an anticapitalist alternative to the global neoliberal onslaught, is the extent to which it is driven from below by explicitly socialist mass organizations with deep-seated democratic impulses. The historical experiences and agency of the TCC and other civic organizations since the early 2000s have created extraordinarily promising engines for change as compared to similar organizations elsewhere in the world.

Above, Thembelihle resident in front of his shack; *below*, Thembelihle residents relaxing in their shack. (Photos by Trevor Ngwane.)

Chapter 2

Against All Odds

The "Spirit of Marikana" and the Resurgence
of the Working-Class Movement in South Africa[1]

Trevor Ngwane

Introduction

What is the political significance of the police killing of thirty-four miners who
were on strike in Marikana? I think the strike represents a high point in what
are still the early days of the workers' movement resurgence in South Africa. For
a short while the strikers at Lonmin stood heroically at the fore of the workers'
struggle against the bosses, thus becoming a true vanguard of the working-class
struggle. They were rebelling not only against their exploitation at the workplace
but, it seems to me, also against the oppression and misery of substandard living
conditions in the shantytowns of Rustenburg, or what may be called South Africa's "platinum city," where the majority of them live. A wave of strikes followed,
spreading to the gold and coal industries, and in 2014 a strike shut down all the
platinum mines for five months.

The politics behind the Lonmin strike were revolutionary because the
demands were based on what workers actually needed rather than what they
thought the bosses could provide for them. The strikers continued the fight for
several weeks after scores of their comrades were shot dead, injured, or arrested;
the general attitude was that it was better to shut down the mines and *even to die*
than to continue being exploited and oppressed by the mining bosses. "Nothing

29

could be worse than being forced to work and live like this," the workers seemed to be saying. It was more than a strike.

Marikana was about workers risking their jobs and their lives—fighting with collective determination, shared knowledge, and unwavering commitment—for a vision of a life that is different: decent, comfortable, and secure. Revolution happens when millions of workers stand together in united mass action with that vision—a revolutionary vision. This is what I call the "Spirit of Marikana": the combative and inspired movement of workers against all odds.[2]

Class Views of Marikana

Even before the acrid smell of cordite and tear gas had cleared on that fateful sixteenth of August, 2012, conflicting versions and interpretations of the day's events were divided along class lines. The ruling class and its apologists watered down news of the massacre and blamed the workers. The miners themselves, as well as other progressive forces, condemned "those who pulled the trigger and those who pulled the political strings," pointing out that behind the massacre lay "the toxic collusion of capital and the state."[3] The massacre sharply revealed people's loyalties: for or against the capitalist class. Fence sitting is difficult when matters come to a head in such a dramatic fashion; everyone has to choose a side. Unfortunately, the fact of the massacre itself distracted the public from learning the details of how the movement was organized, how it carried on in the wake of the massacre, and how it eventually ended in victory for the workers. The workers vowed to continue the struggle until the demand for R12,500 was won, saying that this was imperative in order to assuage the spirits of the dead and ensure they had not died in vain. This aspect of the Spirit of Marikana led the miners to go on strike again in 2014, behind the same demand.

The 2012 strike was organized and led by a strike committee that the workers elected from among their own ranks. Historically, workers have created their own forms of organization, outside and often against their unions and parties, during rapid upsurges of rank-and-file resistance or in revolutionary situations (Cohen 2011; Barker 2008). It is this "organic capacity" of the working class that I wish to highlight—that is, the ability of workers to fight for their needs and in the process displace established mediatory mechanisms by their spontaneous, autonomous actions (Ness and Azzellini 2011). The fight was led by and the process embodied in the strike committee, which can be viewed as an alternative "workers' council structure [that] is 'spontaneously' generated because it immediately answers the organizational needs of grassroots struggle" (Cohen 2011, 48).

What is necessary as a condition for working-class emancipation and the over-throw of the capitalist state is a well-rounded struggle that unites workplace and community struggles and overcomes the rifts between the economic, the social, and the political (Ness and Azzellini 2011, 7). The following section provides the context in which workers at Marikana went on strike in 2012 and again in 2014, highlighting the ways in which capitalist exploitation of workers has continued in the post-apartheid period, particularly in the mines.

Exploitation of Workers in the Post-apartheid Mines

Capital in the Twenty-First Century, Thomas Piketty's unlikely best seller analyzing growing inequality under capitalism, opens with a reference to the Marikana massacre. Despite some shortcomings in Piketty's treatment of the event (see Alexander 2014a), he nevertheless sees Marikana's importance as a symbol of the direct and tragic clash of capitalist and working-class interests in a global context where the rich are getting richer and the poor poorer. Neoliberal restructuring worldwide has led to workers losing many of the gains made in the postwar period. In a South Africa just emerging from apartheid rule and hardly recovered from it, workers had to weather the storm of the ANC government's neoliberal economic policies. They won some rights, including the vote and the right to strike, but these newfound rights had hardly had time to make a difference before workers had to face the onslaught of privatization, outsourcing, labor flexibility, removal of exchange controls, and other neoliberal attacks (see Bond 2000; Terreblanche 2012). Soon post-apartheid South Africa became the most unequal country in the world. Unemployment went through the roof. Precariousness at work increased, and the cheap labor system fashioned under apartheid continued in mining and other sectors of the economy. Living conditions in working-class areas did not improve, with many workers forced to live in shantytowns that mushroomed for want of housing in the urban areas. Rustenburg, the capital city of platinum production in South Africa, has become the capital city of shantytowns.

Rustenburg is located seventy miles northwest of Johannesburg. Shack settlements pepper the landscape, often found next to mine shafts or adjacent to built-up working-class townships. According to census data, in 2011 the Rustenburg Local Municipality had an estimated population of 549,575, occupying an area of 1,322 square miles (Statistics South Africa 2011). Population growth there is higher than the national average, estimated to have ranged between 3.6% and 15% from the year 2000 to the present. This is due to migration by job seekers from within South Africa—only 7% of migrants originate from other southern African countries like Mozambique, Malawi, Swaziland, or Lesotho (Kibet 2013).

Poverty levels are high in Rustenburg, with 50% of the population recording zero monthly income, 11% earning less than R800, and 38% recording less than R3,200 (R1 is equivalent to about 70 US cents); only 64.7% of the eligible workforce is employed, mostly in the mining sector (Rustenburg Local Municipality 2011, 18). Other sectors of the economy are dependent on mining. The area grows good citrus, but agricultural activity "has been in constant decline due to pollution from mining processes" (Kibet 2013, 70). The termination of the apartheid regime's subsidized regional industrialization program led to great job losses that were exacerbated by the mining sector's adoption of flexible production systems.[4] At the end of the 1990s the number of unemployed migrants swelled, with "100,000 living in informal backyard and shack settlements" (Mosiane 2011, 42). Rising poverty levels saw "the crime rate . . . increasing at a frightening pace" (Kibet 2013, 71). Rising unemployment levels have resulted in "an even more desperate reserve army of labour than in the early days of migrancy" (Forrest 2014, 161), creating conditions for the continuation of the super-exploitation of labor. The intrusion of labor brokers into the centralized employment system run by the recruitment company Teba, along with the increasing employment of locals rather than migrants and various other labor-cost-saving machinations on the part of mining capital, has resulted in "unacceptably low wages, poor conditions and low union levels [affecting] at least a third of labour hired by mines" (Forrest 2014, 165).

Since the end of apartheid and the growth of the unions, in particular the National Union of Mineworkers (NUM), there have been some major gains for miners in South Africa, including significant wage increases, better job security, and eradication of racist policies (Forrest 2014; Bezuidenhout and Buhlungu 2011). However, the mine owners have been reluctant to share their earnings with the workforce. The platinum boom of the 2000s brought enormous profits, benefiting shareholders and executives while labor received very little: "Between 2000 and 2008 workers at South Africa's three largest platinum producers [Anglo American Platinum, Lonmin, and Impala] received only 29% of value added produced," whereas on average during this period labor's share of the value added in South Africa was about 50% (Bowman and Isaacs 2014, 5). The bosses have also sought and found ways to perpetuate the cheap labor system. Generally, "contradictions in the implementation of post-apartheid transformative legislation has resulted in a continued hyperexploitation of both local and non–South African labour" (Forrest 2014, 156).

The use of migrant workers continues to form the cornerstone of the cheap labor system, albeit with some changes (for example, there has been a shift away from employing workers from other countries).[5] Central recruitment of labor has been modified, and the new order allows workers free movement and the ability to seek employment wherever they wish; this has tended, in the context of high unemployment levels and deteriorating economic conditions in rural areas, to ensure mining capital a steady and plentiful supply of skilled and unskilled labor, from which it can pull on its own terms. The power of capital over labor has also been increased by the move toward the use of labor brokers and contracting out in the employment of workers, which fragments the labor force into permanent and contract workers (Bezuidenhout and Buhlungu 2011). There is evidence that "mines use brokers for various reasons, an important one being to circumvent unions. . . . Brokers know that discouraging union membership is the key to sustaining low wages so that they can offer competitive rates to mines whilst securing their own profits" (Forrest 2014, 158). This has undermined labor solidarity and, together with the high competition for jobs, has rendered both groups of workers, permanent and contract, precarious given capital's advantage in the situation.[6]

The NUM has responded ineffectively and sometimes badly to this threat of labor fragmentation. A 2004 report from the union secretariat (quoted in Bezuidenhout and Buhlungu 2008, 278) reveals that mid-level union leaders, when faced with retrenchments, use contract workers as sacrificial lambs to save union members. The NUM has only managed to recruit 10% of subcontracted workers, despite their increasingly high numbers in the sector (Bezuidenhout and Buhlungu 2008).

Bezuidenhout and Buhlungu (2008) have argued that the NUM's success at recruiting workers in the apartheid era failed to translate into the new democratic order for a number of structural and political reasons. One of these was the new upward mobility of worker leaders: becoming a full-time shaft steward now meant a ticket to a high salary and an office job, which included being sent by the company to attend university courses. The bosses also started using shaft stewards as a pool from which to recruit foremen and managers. The practice over time has resulted in the union taking over or having an influence on recruitment processes. Such practices have in some instances led to corruption. The activities of the union leaders introduced social distance between rank-and-file workers and trade union leaders (Buhlungu 2010). Workers had to advance beyond the union to defend their own interests.

It was in the context of disillusion with the union that workers at Lonmin embarked on a strike without the blessing and against the advice of the NUM.

Bezuidenhout and Buhlungu correctly identify the structural and political factors that lie behind this disillusion, including the real failure of the union to effectively defend the interests of workers. But they lack a unified concept that captures the essence of these processes. They correctly note how the union increasingly became a stepping-stone for would-be political and business leaders—with some, such as general secretaries Cyril Ramaphosa and Kgalema Motlante (and more recently Gwede Mantashe) becoming secretaries-general for the ANC and deputy presidents of the country, and some, like Ramaphosa and Marcel Golding, becoming billionaire business owners (Bezuidenhout and Buhlungu 2008). Other structural factors they mention as having eroded the old union solidarity are the demise of the hostel system, which had made it easy for the NUM to organize workers in their living spaces and had created the possibility of upward and occupational mobility, and the entry of women workers into the mining sector. What is unclear in their analysis is how the structural and political factors are related to each other. What is missing in their analysis, I submit, is the concept of the "politics of class collaboration" that informs the political and strategic choices and trajectories of the NUM leadership both in their day-to-day and long-term practice. As Martin Legassick (2007, xxvi) has pointed out, *agency* (that is, leadership and organization) is primary, because consciousness does not mechanically reflect the objective conditions. I will turn to this idea later in the paper, after dealing with the question of the conditions in which workers live and the spaces in which they organize.

Oppression in Workers' Living Spaces

"Ironically," Bezuidenhout and Buhlungu (2008, 265) observe, "the hostel system that was used as a form of near totalitarian labor control [under apartheid] became the organizational fulcrum of many of the union's activities." This observation points to the importance of the workers' living spaces and their link to the workplace in the workers' struggle against the bosses. Because the workers were concentrated in single-sex compounds and hostels, sleeping and eating together, once the NUM had made inroads into the workforce and become a presence in these spaces, union mobilization, communication, and solidarity were greatly facilitated. Indeed, the hostels' public address systems were used to call union meetings. This was an instance of union politics and strategy successfully turning on its head the mining bosses' plan to suppress union organization and labor militancy through the totalitarian hostel system. Bezuidenhout and Buhlungu see the demise of the hostel system as giving rise to an organizing problem for the

NUM because when workers moved out to live in the shantytowns and villages that surround the mines, "the task of mobilizing workers [was] no longer a simple matter of getting every worker out of his or her dormitory to the stadium to listen to speeches and participate in singing" (Bezuidenhout and Buhlungu 2008, 283). This observation suggests that the NUM might have taken shortcuts in its choice of organizing methods; it also reveals a privileging of structure over agency in the authors' analysis. It is not primarily the hostel structure that explains the success or otherwise of organizing. This becomes clear when we consider that during the 2014 platinum strike the bosses could not (as they did during strikes in 1987 and earlier) use the devastating weapon of firing all the workers and closing down the hostels, thus forcing workers to go back to their distant homes in order to crush the strike (Allen 2005, vol. 3). The workers lived in the shack districts of Rustenburg and were able to remain close to the mines during the strike; their living spaces were outside the reach of the bosses' power.

Nevertheless, the point above still underlines the importance of the workers' living spaces. A consideration of workers' lives in the informal settlements is important in understanding the Marikana massacre. The scrapping of apartheid's influx control laws saw workers flocking into the towns and cities in search of employment and economic opportunities. The migration into Rustenburg put pressure on available resources in the town, especially housing: 17.6% of the population is officially estimated to live in the town's twenty-four informal settlements (Rustenburg Local Municipality 2011).[7] The desire for some control over personal space and the option to live with or be visited by kith and kin are the reasons why workers moved out of the hostels into the informal settlements. The mining companies agreed to pay a "living-out allowance" to compensate for the added expenses that workers took on when they left compounds where food and accommodation were subsidized by the employer. This "freedom" turned out to be contradictory in that many workers ended up using the allowance to supplement their meager wages, "cut[ting] their costs to the bone so as to save up money to return to their rural homesteads" (Bezuidenhout and Buhlungu 2010, 252). Greater freedom in fact was bestowed upon and enjoyed by the bosses, who through paying the living-out allowance thereby washed their hands of any responsibility for providing decent living conditions for their workers. The following description of life in one shack settlement in Rustenburg underlines this self-absolution by capital.

The settlement of Nkaneng, also known as Bleskop, is located southeast of Rustenburg on land that is zoned for "agricultural" use and owned by the Royal Bafokeng Administration.[8] *Nkaneng* is Sesotho for "by force," a reference to the establishment of the settlement by way of a land invasion in 1994.[9] It is also called Bleskop because it is situated next to the Bleskop Vertical Shaft, which is owned by Anglo American Platinum (Amplats). The settlement consists of approximately four thousand structures and has an estimated population of 11,879, with most of the residents coming from the Eastern Cape (Rustenburg Local Municipality 2011). Very close to the settlement in a southwesterly direction is the Bleskop compound or hostel. The settlement is on flat ground to the west of a hill and is situated about two miles away from Photsaneng, a small, old, formal township that is partly controlled by the Royal Bafokeng Administration.

The settlement is poorly serviced, lacking electricity, proper sanitation, running water, and community facilities. The road infrastructure is poor, laid out in a grid format where each shack has its own yard. The shacks are mostly made of corrugated iron. Poverty and uncertainty about the future of the settlement discourage residents from using brick and mortar for building; there is a hope that the state will one day build houses for the informal settlement dwellers. Some shacks have ventilated pit toilets courtesy of a government project that ran out of funds before completion, provoking allegations of corruption. Water is ferried into the settlement. At certain times you can see residents queuing with their containers, waiting for the water truck. Several green, stationary water tanks are elevated above the ground and look over the settlement like giant sentinels; these are mostly locked. Privately owned *bakkies* (small trucks) roam the settlement's roads selling water to community members. The advantage to that system is that you get the water at your gate. Since there is no electricity, people rely on wood, coal, and paraffin for their energy. At night it is very dark because there are no street lights.

There are no community facilities such as halls, sports fields, or parks. Community gatherings and meetings are held in an open space marked by a thorn tree in the midst of shacks. Church services are conducted inside people's shacks (some are built slightly bigger than normal for the purpose). There are a few ramshackle general stores built from brick and mortar; there are numerous *spaza* shops in the form of shacks that have a big "window" on a side wall that acts as a counter. A handful of shacks housing small businesses (a hair salon, a tailor, a fruit stand) form a row on the settlement's eastern boundary, across the tarred road that leads to the compound. During the 2012 strike at Amplats all the dozen business shacks located there were burned down, and these were the only ones that reemerged.

Many people entertain themselves by playing the radio, visiting each other, drinking in the local *shebeens,* or taking a walk across the railway line to Photsaneng, which has a motor vehicle service station, a money lending establishment, and a couple of shops that sell household items (meat and beer can be bought and consumed on shop premises). Boarding a passing minibus taxi takes you east into the city of Rustenburg or, if you like, west to the small town of Marikana, where there are more shops and a livelier hustle and bustle than in Photsaneng.

The people who live in the area represent a cross section of the working class. The majority appear to be unemployed, self-employed, and/or underemployed workers. Mine jobs are preferred, but the increasing use of labor brokers exposes mineworkers to precariousness (Forrest 2014). Unlike during the days of apartheid, "the informal sector is a dominating presence in the lives" of migrant workers today (Cox, Hemson, and Todes 2004, 12). Many residents can be regarded as migrants in that they maintain ties with their homes and families in the rural areas.[10] However, many recent migrants have not been able to secure formal employment and find themselves "in an increasingly marginal position economically, reliant on informal activities, or on poorly paid and insecure work in the formal sector (e.g., security and domestic work)" (Cox, Hemson, and Todes 2004, 12). Most come from the "deep rural areas" where poverty levels are high and employment prospects slim.[11] As a consequence, migrants find themselves engaging in a range of activities more accurately regarded as "livelihoods" than "employment," the same activities that are "crucially employed by the majority in the global south to adapt to changing social and economic conditions" (Mosiane 2011, 39; Rakodi 1995).

It can be surmised that living in these terrible conditions provided some of the pressure and motivation that steeled the resolve of the striking Lonmin workers to fight to win and to the bitter end. It should also be noted that many miners maintain two households: one in the shack settlement, where they might be living with a wife or girlfriend or relative, and the other at the rural homestead where the extended family lives. This splits the wage two ways and across a wide geographical space. Some miners live with their children in the shacks while maintaining their rural homes for stability, loyalty, culture, and a place to retire. These ties to the rural home have sometimes confused theorists about the class identity of migrants. As it is usually articulated, the theory of modes of production suggests that the rural area represents a peasant way of life and as such is precapitalist in essence; the migrant thus "oscillates" between two worlds and two modes of production, feudal or tributary and capitalist (see Wolpe 1972). Recent Marxist analyses of this question differ with this interpretation and suggest that capitalism can and in fact always has used different forms of labor exploitation, cultural practices, and political arrangements, as long as these operate within its logic and are subject to its laws of motion (see Banaji 2010). The miners of

Rustenburg are proletarians who must struggle to make a life in the context of a complex reality that is constituted by underlying processes driven by the uneven and combined development of capitalism (Ashman 2012).

Organization in Worker Living Spaces

Since informal settlements are invariably established without the state's approval or support and often against its wishes, the inhabitants have to organize themselves in order to have basic services such as water and sanitation, and to maintain a semblance of order and peaceful social living. As a result, in almost all of South Africa's informal settlements there are people's committees. These are formed by the community independently of the authorities and can be regarded as "civic" in that they aspire to take care of the affairs of the community as a whole, claiming authority over the community and acting as a kind of improvised government. In Nkaneng, as has often happened in other informal settlements, it was the original people's committee that helped establish the settlement through, in this case, a 1994 land invasion that was peaceful and relatively uncontested by the authorities. The land invasion coincided with the demise of apartheid and the extension of the franchise to all.

This first committee formed around the leader of the invasion, an unemployed worker called Cairo, and concerned itself with allocating stands and setting up a basic social and political framework for a new settlement. However, Cairo's committee was soon displaced by a leadership drawn from among the employed miners that was known as Five Madoda, a civic structure or "vigilante committee" linked to the Mouthpiece Workers Union. The political contestation of workers' residential space was linked to the struggle for power between this union and NUM; the NUM dominated the hostels to such an extent that in reality workers living therein had no choice but to join it. Five Madoda appears to have organized itself in the nearby Bleskop hostel, from which it took control of the settlement and became a sovereign civic authority. The new union was formed in 1997 and came to be recognized by the bosses as a rival of the NUM. Its rise happened during a time of confusion and turmoil at Amplats, which was caused by the unbundling of JCI (the parent company) as well as workers' fears and their militant action to defend their provident fund benefits. The formation and growth of the new union was accompanied by violence in the platinum belt, including assassinations carried out in the rural areas of the Eastern Cape (Bruce 2001).

Self-organization and self-government in South Africa's informal settlements during the 1990s—throughout the country a period of violent political turmoil related to the birth pangs of the democratic order—was often accompanied by violent contestation for control of these areas. The committee that took over in Nkaneng, the Five Madoda, was jealous of its rule, and residents were treated as subjects of the committee rather than of the state. For example, police were not allowed into the area; the committee dealt with all disputes and engaged in crime fighting. It also supervised small business operations in the area, including the shebeens. It is apparent that its rule was less democratic or benevolent than Cairo's earlier committee (for example, curfews were imposed on the settlement).

This was a period when Nkaneng was experiencing rapid growth and the state had more or less thrown up its hands and left the informal settlements to their own devices, necessitating the construction of local power centers. Abuse of power, opportunism, and criminality increasingly characterized the rule of Five Madoda. The committee ran a people's court and meted out people's justice in the form of fines and corporal punishment. The Mouthpiece Workers Union also appears to have been led by unsavory characters who involved themselves in criminal activities, including corruption and instigating violence and murder (Bruce 2001).

The Five Madoda was violently driven out of the township when the power of Mouthpiece waned and the residents were at the end of their rope. The committee was replaced by a people's committee that had started operating in parallel fashion during the Five Madoda era. This people's committee, sometimes referred to as a "street committee," seemed to follow in the Five Madoda's footsteps in its muscular control of affairs in the settlement. It, too, focused on crime fighting and running a people's court that later lost credibility in the eyes of some community members due to its alleged partiality and harshness, which included the use of torture. In light of this single-minded focus on security-related functions, some commentators have suggested that a "rural vigilante militarism" was imported from the rural areas and adapted into the life of some urban informal settlements by migrants (Bruce 2001).

Later, the security function was removed from the people's committee and transferred into the Community Policing Forum, a state structure in which police and communities jointly fight against crime (Pelser, Schnetler, and Louw 2002). The street committee was later replaced by a ward committee, a state structure meant to afford residents participation in an advisory capacity in local government matters (Republic of South Africa 2005). Political parties, especially the ANC, now operate in the area. It is clear that the struggle to improve living conditions is often coterminous with attempts to impose law and order upon workers, and the forms of these impositions are dynamic and unstable.

Iinkundla Networks

In Nkaneng-Bleskop, an especially interesting development in community organization has been the rise of a type of committee that is based on homeboy networks, called *iinkundla*. It coexists with the ward committee, the ANC local party committee, and a Community Policing Forum. But recently iinkundla seem to be gaining prominence and influence beyond taking care of matters when someone dies and resolving minor disputes. In a by-election held in 2012 the iinkundla were mobilized to support an independent candidate against an ANC candidate when the local government ward councilor, who is directly elected, passed away. Higher structures in the ANC attempted to impose their own candidate on the local branch as a result of factionalism in the party. This provoked a rebellion in which the branch's preferred candidate, the local chairperson of the ANC Youth League, put himself forward as an independent and won the seat from the ruling party. The iinkundla threw their weight behind the independent, who has subsequently joined the Economic Freedom Fighters (EFF) of Julius Malema.[12]

The iinkundla system originated in the rural areas of the Eastern Cape, where the chiefs hold court in their homesteads. *Inkundla* literally means an open space like a courtyard and has connotations of transparency or publicness of the proceedings taking place therein. It is here that decisions affecting the community or the chief's subjects are made, and here that disputes are resolved. When crime fighting became a harsh organized response under Five Madoda and the civic committee that succeeded it, both of which meted out heavy-handed and sometimes arbitrary justice, people from the Eastern Cape began to use their homeboy networks as dispute resolution mechanisms and as a way of protecting their "homies" from falling into the jurisdiction of the committee courts. The idea was that the iinkundla would deal with the wrongdoing of people who came from back home in Bizana, Ngqeleni, Mount Frere, and other Eastern Cape rural areas, mostly in the former Republic of Transkei. This reversion to a rural, "traditional" form of organization and justice underlines the relevance of the rural in the urban and demonstrates the survival of cultural and juridical practices and values that belong to an earlier way of life or are associated with precapitalist modes of production. Are these people torn between the old and the new? Or are they comfortably semi-urban, living in the urban areas while maintaining an essentially rural or traditionalist value system?

The deployment of iinkundla networks to gain political support for the independent candidate suggests that these questions miss an important point. They are based on viewing the modern and the traditional in a dichotomous fashion—as if they exist in separate worlds and, when they do meet or coexist, operate according to different logics. This approach is consonant with a modernization-theory perspective. This theory sees all societies as moving from traditional to modern. Where traditional attributes exist, it is assumed to be only a matter of time before they disappear and are replaced by the new. The concept of articulation is deployed to explain the relationship of the old and the new in instances where these coexist. This approach is often found in early interpretations of the political economy of South Africa, such as Harold Wolpe's "cheap labour thesis" (whereby two modes of production, the capitalist and the precapitalist, "articulate" in the form of the migrant labor system, thus realizing the superexploitation of labor). But if we view historical development as a multilinear rather than a unilinear process, then we will realize, as Banaji argues, that the laws of motion of the capitalist mode of production find ways of subsuming earlier economic and social forms into the logic of capital (Banaji 2010). Hence, the iinkundla system is not so much a return to the rural areas and traditional ways as the use and adaptation of these ways to new purposes in the city. Exactly how and why this happens are empirical questions that can best be answered through research guided by the correct theoretical framework; but first we must look at the other side of worker self-organization, which is organization within the workplace itself.

Organizing the Fightback at the Workplace

The most important thing about the Lonmin strike that precipitated the Marikana massacre is that it was led by the workers themselves and not their union, the NUM. Indeed, the NUM distanced itself from the strike and publicly condemned it. The workers refused to listen to the union's admonitions, reflecting their distrust and unhappiness with the NUM and precipitating their break with it. Workers at Impala Platinum had been the first to embark on a strike that was hostile to the union, several months before the Lonmin strike. The Lonmin strikers formed a similar strike committee to lead and organize their action. They put forward the demand for R12,500 per month, which gained popularity among the workers. The strike that began as a rebellion of the rock drill operators (RDOs) soon spread, until it was supported by all the workers on the mine.

The strike committee was elected by the workers. It called regular meetings of the strikers, kept the strike together by instilling discipline and politics, and attempted to negotiate with management. Initially the strikers held their meetings at the company stadium next to the compound. Later, workers were refused access to the stadium and met at a sports field next to the Nkaneng-Wonderkop settlement or on the mountain where the shootings took place during the massacre. The move to the mountain was precipitated by a violent skirmish involving some strikers and NUM local leaders, after the workers marched to the union office. The mountain, because of its elevation, provided a better vantage point from which to observe attacks against the workers.

The story of the massacre has been told in detail in a book by Peter Alexander and a documentary film by Rehad Desai (Alexander et al. 2012; Desai 2014). Here I would like to note how the self-organization of the strikers before and after the massacre was surprisingly strong and resilient; the strike at no point showed any serious signs of flagging despite a relentless onslaught by the bosses and the state, who used a variety of tactics aimed at dividing and weakening the strike. The workers met every day on the mountain in the days leading up to the massacre and every day on the sports field after it. The impression I got when I attended one of these meetings—two days after the massacre—was of discipline, determination, and respect. Some leading members of the strike committee, such as Mgcineni "Mambush" Noki, the man with the green blanket, had died under a hail of bullets; new workers took their places. No one was allowed to wear a hat at the meeting, in deference to the dead. Yet the trauma of the massacre appeared to have only strengthened the workers' resolve and increased their realization that unity was the key to victory.

Outsiders, including the media, were allowed to attend the general meeting and were directed to the committee if necessary. The meeting was already in session as we met with the committee itself on the edges of the bigger group, sitting on the ground in a small, tight circle to speak with the strike leaders. The strike meeting welcomed messages of support and encouragement and in this respect had to break its rules that prevented females attending and addressing the male gathering. There was a lot of singing when the workers came to and left the meeting in groups. Workers' power was tangible in the very breath that we took.[13]

The full story of what happened during the massacre has yet to be told. The commission set up by the South African government has, after two years, completed its work and submitted its report, whose conclusions and recommendations have proven controversial (Alexander 2014). However, some facts seem to be indisputable: the police were ordered by the powers that be to violently crush the strike and proceeded to do this, hunting down fleeing workers like animals and shooting some who were cowering among the mountain's huge boulders as they tried to hide from the police helicopters, armored cars, and sharpshooters. Some workers bled to death lying on the ground as the police kept medical help at bay.[14] There was close cooperation and connivance between the state and capital in the repression of the strike; Lonmin lent its helicopter and jail facilities to the police. Evidence suggests that one worker was shot in the back by police at long range as he scrambled across a small stream in a desperate bid to escape; this evidence was not contested during the Farlam Commission hearings. On the day of the massacre, four mortuary vans were brought to the scene *before* it happened, together with thousands of rounds of live ammunition: the massacre was planned (Alexander 2014).

The strike went on for several weeks after the massacre before the bosses relented and granted increases of up to 22% for certain categories of workers. The demand for R12,500 (US$850) a month was not met, but it became a rallying cry in the wave of strikes that broke out in the South African platinum, gold, and coal mines for several months after the massacre. A strike broke out at Amplats, the biggest platinum mine, and it too was led by a workers' strike committee. The workers subsequently joined the Association of Mineworkers and Construction Union (AMCU) en masse, deserting the NUM. In 2014, from their new home, they launched a five-month-long strike against all three platinum mining companies that involved 70,000 workers and demanded the R12,500. This time, the strike was conducted according to the regulations of the Labour Relations Act and as such was "protected," with the bosses unable to fire the workers willy-nilly. By joining AMCU the workers sought the power and safety of the "union of the office," the better to take forward the demands formulated during the struggles led by the "union of the mountain." Even during the so-called wildcat strikes that first broached the R12,500 demand, and certainly in the course of the orderly five-month strike, relentless propaganda by the state and capital against the workers' demands failed to suppress the solidarity that the broader working class felt with the strikers. The platinum strikers appear to have won the sympathy of millions and millions of ordinary workers by their struggle.

NUM leadership, including that of the Congress of South African Trade Unions (COSATU) and the South African Communist Party (SACP), came out on the side of the police who shot the strikers. The strikers provoked the police, they said; the demand was unrealistic; the strike threatened orderly labor relations; and so on. A campaign of slander was waged against AMCU, labeling it a vigilante union that used violence to recruit (Tabane 2013). So Bezuidenhout and Buhlungu's identification of structural and political factors leading to the decline of the NUM, and indeed of COSATU, misses a crucial point: namely, that it is above all the politics of class collaboration that explains the impending demise of these once-powerful trade union organizations. The hallmark of the politics of class collaboration is a lack of faith in the power of the working class to lead the struggle against the bosses and win. It is a failure to see workers as the embodiment of the solution to the problems of humanity that emanate from capitalism. Leaders of class collaboration tend to be enamored with the power of the bosses, and their bedazzlement blinds them to the power of the workers. They cannot see the gold under their noses, in their own meetings, down the streets where they live; they can only see the capitalists' tinsel and be impressed by the high swivel chairs found in their boardrooms. They look for solutions everywhere except in the working class. Worker leaders unfortunately seek a path between the interests of the workers and the bosses, seeking accommodation between the classes rather than leading the struggle of oppressed against oppressor.

At the level of the state this politics takes forms like social democracy and Stalinism. The ANC government consists of social democrats, Stalinists, and neoliberals. In practice, the global economic crisis blurs the lines of demarcation between these political ideologies. The Stalinists and the social democrats seek a rapprochement between the bosses who benefited from apartheid capitalism and the workers who suffered under it. In this respect they disagree with the neoliberals, whose raison d'être is to trample on workers' interests. At the workplace, union leaders have become adept at balancing the interests of the bosses with those of the workers—a futile exercise given the ongoing capitalist crisis.

Bezuidenhout and Buhlungu's research, as noted above, suggests that the so-called understanding between the union and the bosses, on balance and over time, has served largely to undermine the NUM's ability to defend and promote its members' interests. This is the thing about the politics of class collaboration. One day it preaches wage restraint in the interest of profits and realism. The next it's about supporting a capitalist government that is supposedly worker-friendly, and the day after that it condones a police massacre of workers on strike for a living wage. August 16, 2012, was just another day in the politics of class collaboration.[15]

Theoretical and Strategic Implications

The discussion of workers' control at the workplace and in their living space raises a number of theoretical and strategic issues for the workers' movement. First, there is a need to consider the alternative forms of political organization that the workers create. During revolutionary upheavals, soviet-type worker organizations, which often traverse industrial and residential districts, are formed by mobilized workers (see Barker 1995, 2008). However, as we have seen in the discussion above, it is possible in less revolutionary periods to identify two major forms of these organs of worker control and coordination of struggle: namely, those that operate at the workplace and those that operate at the living space. On the one hand there are workers' councils and other autonomous self-management structures that have been formed primarily at the workplace, with the aim of workers taking control of production processes there (see Ness and Azzellini 2011). On the other hand there are the neighborhood councils, civic organizations, and other autonomous community-based structures that organize in the spaces where workers live.[16] From a theoretical perspective, the latter have not been consistently approached as instances of worker control, probably because of the recognition that communities are likely to consist of different class elements and not just the proletariat. It is also the case that political parties have tended to occupy the political sphere in workers' living spaces. Yet worker self-organization at the living space still has to be approached from a working-class perspective and be accorded its proper status and place.

Second, and more generally, there is the question of the unity of labor and community struggles. To what extent do worker-control structures that operate at the workplace and at the living space cooperate with each other? This is an empirical and a strategic question. Strategically, the strongest way forward for the workers' movement is to unite the struggles at home and at work. Workers on strike need the support of their communities, including family, friends, neighbors, unemployed workers, youth, and so on. The workers' social revolution is hard to conceive of without changes happening at both the workplace and the living space. What goes on at the living space is very important in building the movement.

The Lonmin strike received support from the residents of Nkaneng-Wonderkop. This was especially true after the massacre, when, for example, the women's group Sikhala Sonke (Zulu for "we are all crying") was formed to organize support for both the miners and their families (SAPA 2013). This organization wrote and performed a play that portrayed the Marikana massacre from the point of view of the miners' families. The strike also had an impact on the local committees of Nkaneng-Wonderkop. The old people's committee affiliated with the South African National Civic Organisation, like COSATU in alliance with the ANC, continued to operate but was eclipsed by a new civic committee that was directly linked to the strike. The local ANC party branch was overtaken by the United Democratic Movement, a political party whose base is in the Eastern Cape, and later and more decisively by the EFF. The ANC lost its popularity in this informal settlement situated next to the mountain where the massacre happened.

During the Impala strike there was also a lot of community support. Workers' meetings traditionally held at the mine hostel were instead held in the local informal settlement, Freedom Park, because the bosses refused to have the meetings on company premises. The meetings became community meetings that local residents attended and so were drawn into the strike. More than in any other strike in South Africa in the post-apartheid era, the platinum strikes seem to have begun to bridge the gap between community and labor struggles.

The views and analyses presented in this paper take as their premise the assumption that the working class is the revolutionary subject—that is, workers constitute the class that has the organic capacity to lead the struggle for human emancipation (Marx 1844). This assumption seems to hold when we analyze what happened at Marikana: how the workers, on their own and without the support of their union, waged a struggle that shook the mining capitalists and made history. It is true that the Lonmin strike itself was the culmination of a series of struggles that signaled increasing combativeness in the working class. Several other important struggles preceded it. There was the burgeoning movement of community protests called "service delivery protests," which steadily increased in frequency over the past decade (Runciman, Ngwane, and Alexander 2012). And in 2007 and 2010 there were two major strikes by public sector workers, the biggest in the history of the country (Ceruti 2011). The political message of these strikes to the millions of workers watching was that it is okay to strike against "your own government." Marikana was, however, a turning point (Alexander 2013). It was a critical event and an encounter that provoked "new forms of consciousness and political imagination in South Africa."[17] After Marikana, the workers' struggle will never be the same again.

The fall of the NUM as the majority union in the platinum mines (it lost tens of thousands of its members to the AMCU) had the consequence of eroding its power in COSATU, thus adding grist to the mill of unionists beginning to vocalize their doubts about the strategic wisdom of subordinating organized labor to the politics of the ANC-SACP-COSATU alliance. The National Union of Metalworkers of South Africa (NUMSA), the biggest union in COSATU, held a special congress in 2013 in which it decided to pull out of the alliance and withhold election support for the ANC. During the congress workers spontaneously and out of their pockets donated more than R100,000 to the Marikana widows in an emotional outpouring of solidarity.[18] NUMSA has subsequently formed a united front that seeks to unite labor and community struggles and serve as a stepping-stone toward the formation of a working-class party (Ashman and Pons-Vignon 2015). Julius Malema was the first influential politician to offer a public pledge of solidarity with the Lonmin strike. He launched his party, the EFF, at the mountain where the massacre took place—a party that would dramatically change public views of the South African parliament and its political alignments.

Marikana gave rise to a new mood of defiance and determination among ordinary people in struggle in South Africa. Many land invasions and house occupations that happened in the period after the massacre were named Marikana: the occupation of government houses in Mzimhlophe, Soweto; the informal settlement born of a land invasion in Philippi, Cape Town; the informal settlement born of a land invasion in Tlokwe, Potchefstroom; and more. Clearly Marikana grabbed the popular imagination as a struggle that showed determination, steadfastness, and a willingness to risk all. "We are not moving here; they must kill us as they killed the people in Marikana" is a common refrain among workers in struggle at the workplace or living space. There is a new confidence and hope, a sense of doing things ourselves, a sense that through struggle victory is possible.

The country has seen an increase in the number of community protests, with these becoming increasingly militant in the face of a heavy-handed response by the police. The demobilization and demoralization that set in during the past twenty years of "freedom," including the stultifying grip of the politics of class collaboration, is slowly being shaken off. Despite the separation between community and labor struggles, and the fact that these are as yet early days, developments suggest that the workers' movement is again in motion in South Africa. The support that Lonmin and Impala strikers received from their informal settlement communities has planted the seeds for the unification of labor and community struggles. Working-class agency is in the process of being recovered, and the organic capacity of the working class, long suppressed, is being released.[19]

Conclusion

The working-class movement has two legs: struggles at the workplace and struggles at the living space. The Marikana massacre highlights the importance of self-organization at the workers' living space. There is a real possibility of uniting labor and community struggles in South Africa and in other countries, and of forging a revolutionary workers' movement that will lead society out of the morass of the current global capitalist economic crisis. The capitalist class has no solution for the crisis; their focus is on how to manage it, but they are not even in agreement about how to do this. The events at Marikana brought out the organic capacity of the working class. They instilled new hope and heralded a new confidence, giving birth to the Spirit of Marikana. It is this spirit that socialists must protect, nurture, and develop as we move forward, led by workers in struggle.

Above, Nkaneng informal settlement with Karee minehead in the background; *below*, shacks at Nkaneng informal settlement. (All photos for this chapter by Trevor Ngwane.)

Above, domestic scene at Enkanini informal settlement, Wonderkop, next to the site of the Marikana massacre; *below*, leaders of the community committee at Freedom Park informal settlement, Rustenburg

Chapter 3

Makoko Slum Settlement

Migrant Peasants on the Lagos Lagoon, Nigeria

Ayokunle Olumuyiwa Omobowale
with Adefemi Abdulmojeed Adeyanju

Introduction

Strategically placed on the west coast of Nigeria and enjoying the preference of industries, investors, and development right from the colonial era, Lagos state, with a total land mass of about 1,290 square miles, attracts a huge population from across Nigeria and the West African coast (Agbola and Agunbiade [2007] 2009; Gandy 2006). According to Agbola and Agunbiade ([2007] 2009), the land mass of Lagos state is just 0.4% of the total land mass of Nigeria, which is estimated at 386,000 square miles. Yet it is home to 7% of Nigeria's people: the nation has a population of over 170 million, about 12 million of whom live in Lagos. Though relatively more industrialized than the rest of the country, Lagos is subject to the impact of population pressure, and many Lagos residents end up in slums, surviving in the lower rungs of the proletarian class (Agbola and Agunbiade [2007] 2009). Continual migration into Lagos and, of course, infringement on urban planning rules and regulations have resulted in the emergence of slums across the landscape of the state (Nubi and Ajoku 2011; Castles 2009; Adepoju 2002).

One such slum is Makoko, strategically located on and around the Lagos Lagoon, providing an easy proximity to Lagos Island, the state's economic and commercial epicenter. Established as a fishing settlement in the eighteenth century, Makoko is divided into two sections: the land Makoko and the lagoon

Makoko (the latter being the primary focus of this research). Whereas the land Makoko is predominantly inhabited by members of the Yoruba proletarian class, who are mostly junior workers on Lagos Island, the lagoon Makoko is predominantly inhabited by migrant peasants from across Nigeria and the West African coast, living in stilt houses (Ayeni 2014; Adelekan 2010). This study examines the resilience of (lagoon) Makoko as a deprived proletarian settlement of migrant peasants. While specifically focusing on the context of migrations, the social organization of stilt housing, and the challenges and survival tactics of Makoko settlers, this paper views the settlement's active agency as what maintains the social structure of the community.

Most literature limits slum studies to the realm of deprived, broken-down infrastructure. Slums are portrayed as diseased, poor, and crime-ridden, in need of development intervention.[1] They are a global phenomenon, relative in nature, and more commonplace in the Global South. Pokhariyal (2010, 61–62) gave a succinct description of the slum:

> Unemployment and/or poor remuneration for the employed can be one of the main compelling factors to take shelter in slums. Slums often come into existence in the vicinity of the places and organizations providing employment opportunities to the lower strata of the workforce. This saves vital man-hours as well as the transportation cost from the settlement to the place of work. In this manner, the residents of the slums divert some of their limited financial resources to procure other additional utilities, which they could not probably afford, if moved to relatively better settlements. This seems to be one of the reasons for continued living in the slums for some of the residents. In some cases land once owned by people, which was providing them shelter and livelihood, is taken by the government for social and economic activities or for allocation to private enterprises. These residents are neither provided adequate compensation for their lands nor given alternative land which could make resettlement feasible. Hence, they are made landless due to alleged corruption and lack of ethical and moral values . . . amongst officials and politicians. However, the situation of slums varies from city to city depending upon overall population, employment potential, and the cost of living in the particular city.

Beyond the "deprived" discourses, however, it is important to understand the slum environment as an active agency. The structures, social relations, power limitations, and power relations, as well as the exchange system, are the social processes that sustain an otherwise precarious environment. Thus, Parnell's (2003) research elaborately described the formation of inner-city slum yards in Johannesburg between 1910 and 1923. Though described as filthy, this pre-apartheid slum settlement provided expensive accommodation for the proletarian workers of gold mining companies in Johannesburg. The slum was thus a wealth creator for some property owners within the working-class slum environment. Meschkank's (2011) research on poverty tourism in the Dharavi slum in Mumbai, India, traces the history of "slumming" to the leisure touring of slum areas of London by the elite class in the nineteenth century. Contemporary slum tourism is a commercialized enterprise that conveys the privileged class around slum areas to observe and construct realities of peasanthood in the modern world. Meschkank notes that whereas the "commercialization of poverty as a tourist commodity is [often] criticized as voyeurism and exploitation" (47–48), it is interesting to note how tourist agents reconstruct the social reality of the slum to their clients in such a way as to minimize the "poverty" thesis. The tourism agents thus redescribe the Dharavi slum as "a place of poverty and hardship but also a place of enterprise, humor and non-stop activity" (56), emphasizing Dharavi's more than ten thousand small-scale industries and its yearly transactional value of more than $665 million. Furthermore, Sen (2012) described the involvement of child vigilantes in politics and violence in a highly volatile slum divided between Hindus and Muslims in Hyderabad. Young Muslim boys formed the vigilante group in 2003 to advance the interest of the Muslim population in the Hindu-dominated settlement. Armed with dangerous weapons and ranging in age from nine to fourteen years, the child vigilantes protect and patrol streets, resist Hindu domination, and chastise Muslim residents who interact with the Hindu population.

The literature reviewed above shows that slums are not passive communities but social structures, with their own embedded subcultures, economies, and social realities. Of course, the literature has also described Makoko mostly within the construct of the passive, deprived, poor, and vulnerable slum (see Nubi and Ajoku 2011; Adelekan 2010; Agbola and Agunbiade [2007] 2009). While these negative descriptions are not necessarily unfounded, this chapter describes instead the social reality of lagoon Makoko as a settlement of economically active migrant traders, whose resolve to resist demolition and displacement has kept Makoko standing.

Lagoon Makoko: A Migrant Slum in Precarious Existence

Makoko is one of the oldest surviving slums in the world (Marx, Stoker, and Suri

2012). It has survived through the years as a settlement of migrant peasants who have to sustain survival and present a life of constructed "comfort" to other peasants outside the lagoon Makoko social space. Lagoon Makoko is visible from the Third Mainland Bridge.[2] It is predominantly inhabited by migrants from Nigeria's Niger Delta region and other migrants from Benin, Cameroon, Ghana, and Togo. The population is estimated at about twenty thousand (Udo-Udoma 2014; *Vanguard* 2012).[3] The settlement mostly attracts peasant fishermen, loggers, and other traders to whom the lagoon environment provides a natural access to fish, transportation of wood, and other resources. Makoko residents also engage in salt making, sawmilling, trading, and sand dredging (Udo-Udoma 2014; Agbola and Agunbiade [2007] 2009).

Makoko is surrounded by the more prosperous parts of Lagos; thus, its existence presents an eyesore to its affluent neighbors and the Lagos state government, who would rather have Makoko obliterated. The state government has an urban renewal policy that seeks to transform all slums into more environmentally friendly spaces with humane housing (Okoli 2013). Hence, Makoko is under constant threat of eviction and demolition (Collins 2015; Marx, Stoker, and Suri 2012). On July 12, 2012, after just about seventy-two hours' notice, a huge part of the lagoon Makoko was demolished and a leader of the community who resisted was shot dead by the police (Ibiwoye 2014; BBC 2012). The incident attracted public outcry as a government's attempt to dislodge the poor and redevelop Makoko into an elitist environment for the affluent. The National Human Rights Commission (NHRC) stepped in to investigate forced eviction and cases of human rights abuse that were reported (Okulaja 2013).[4] The intervention of the NHRC (an agency of the federal government) was largely a political gimmick, born out of the competition and animosity between the Peoples' Democratic Party (PDP), which ruled at the federal level, and the All Peoples' Congress (APC), the opposition party that controlled Lagos state. Since the federal government claims control over waterfronts and waterways, Makoko's demolition was put on hold. The stilt houses have been reconstructed, and of course the settlement is booming once again. However, only time will tell how long Makoko might remain, especially now that the APC has won the 2015 presidential and gubernatorial elections and thus controls the federal government and the coercive forces of the state.

Methodology

Lagoon Makoko was selected for this study because it accommodates a huge number of the migrant peasants whose social reality is the primary focus of the study

(Adelekan 2010; Agbola and Agunbiade [2007] 2009). While a negligible number of the residents are Yoruba, the majority are Egun or else migrants from riverine areas of South South Nigeria (especially the Ijaw, Ilaje, Itsekiri, and Urhobo), Benin, Cameroon, Togo, and Ghana.[5] The research design was both exploratory and descriptive. Exploratory design was adopted to uncover taken-for-granted aspects of Makoko social life and experience, while descriptive design quantitatively probed the opinion of residents about life at Makoko (Breslin and Buchanan 2008; Punch 2005). Hence, both quantitative and qualitative data were collected. For the survey, Makoko was clustered into residential and vocational areas. Thereafter, systematic sampling was used to select a total of three hundred samples for the quantitative data, while twenty residents who were either community leaders or had stayed in Makoko for at least ten years were selected for oral interview. Specially designed questionnaires and interview guides were utilized as research instruments. Quantitative data were analyzed into simple percentages, while qualitative data were subjected to content analysis. The researchers received respondents' and interviewees' informed consent and have protected their identity and interests in order to uphold ethical standards.

The Socio-demographics

This section presents the socio-demographic characteristics of respondents. Socio-demographic characteristics are important because they give credence to the social experience of research subjects for articulate inference in the explanation of social reality (Nwizu et al. 2011; Hayes 2000). This section principally presents respondents' age, gender, marital status, education, occupation, and years of residence at Makoko.

Most of the survey respondents were between the ages of 18 and 28 (27.3%), 29 and 39 (17.7%), or 40 and 50 (41%), while the rest were over 50 (14%). These data reveal that the majority of respondents fall within the active years of working age (that is, 18–50). They thus form a part of the working population with youthful strength for economic engagement, and they direct their strength at working as peasant fishermen (41.7%), traders (35%), and wood cutters and processors (28.3%). Furthermore, 80% of the respondents are male. This does not necessarily mean that the margin between the male and female population in Makoko is this huge. The high representation of men in the study is partly due to the systematic sampling procedure that was adopted and the patriarchal nature of the community, which somewhat prevents direct access to married women without their husbands' express consent (Kandiyoti 1988). However, the demographic majority of males in the study is also indicative of the nature of economic division of labor in Makoko, which puts male members of the community in charge of the most vibrant economic activities such as fishing, lumber, sand dredging, and deep-water salt extraction.

The survey also reveals that 81.3% of respondents were married. Among the proletarian class, which has strong traditional marital values, marriage is a normative social institution and mark of respectability, indicative of economic capability and responsibility. Hence, a married male acquires social honor, while a married female is also accorded social respect and would not be viewed as a potential sex worker (Walker 2012; Otoo-Oyortey and Pobi 2003; Chojnacka 2000). This explains the high rate of marriage among residents of the Makoko slum.

In terms of formal education, the majority—72.7%—had none. Without formal education in the modern system, they are relegated to the lowest strata of society. Forming a part of the proletarian base, the migrant peasants create a slum community with a subculture that is predicated on the social reality of the slum and clings to it, resisting dislocation. The slum location constitutes their entire world of freedom and survival within the competitive and individualist capitalist system of survival of the fittest. The three main occupations that respondents engage in—fishing, trade, and lumber—reflect the educational makeup of the community. Makoko is a major corridor for the lumber trade. Logs travel by water between Makoko and other riverine communities in Nigeria, and the possibility of log smuggling in and out of Nigeria cannot be ruled out. Hence, it is important to note that many of those who claim to be fishers also engage in some form of logging, whether as transporters, cutters, processors, sellers, or possibly smugglers.

Finally, as many as 79% of the respondents claimed they had inhabited Makoko for over sixteen years. Based on the long years of residence of the majority of the inhabitants, they must have developed a strong socio-psychological sense of belonging within the community, with a high degree of ingrained identity. Hence, for them Makoko is not just a trading outpost on the trenches of the lagoon; it is a home and heritage to be protected from the onslaught of the coercive forces of the state and affluent land speculators who may have an interest in getting them dislodged. This somewhat explains the purpose behind the institution of the *Baale* (traditional leader) system in Makoko: to entrench a sort of Yoruba-tradition political system and create and instill the constructions of immemorial aboriginal heritage within the established traditional institutions of the Makoko stilt slum on the Lagos Lagoon (Blier 1985).

Makoko: The Context of Migrations

Most literature on migration discusses people's decisions to migrate especially within the realms of the push and pull factors (Kumar and Sidhu 2005; Hollifield 2004; Hall 2000). As valid as these discourses are, it is important to understand the context of migration beyond push and pull explanations, especially within the context of a slum environment. Migration is a social, relational structure. People are not just pushed and pulled. They move due to constructions of reality based on their interpretation of the situation at the point of departure and point of destination (Castles 2009; Silvey 2006). These constructions provide migrants with reasoned motives to move into lagoon Makoko. An elitist view of Makoko presents a precarious environment inhabited by poverty-stricken members of the proletarian class who have little hope of escaping peasanthood and moving into the privileged classes (Adelekan 2010; Douglas et al. 2008). Of course, Makoko residents may fall within the proletarian category; they do not, however, necessarily consider themselves economically deprived.

Though a slum, Makoko stands out as a center of vibrant economic activities for as many as 91% of the respondents. It provides access to fishing, logging, and other businesses that residents otherwise would have been unable to access or engage in. Hence, the physical state of squalor that Makoko presents to the outside world is very much in conflict with residents' interpretations of its economic vibrancy, just as in the case of the Dharavi slum in India (Nijman 2015; Verma 2012; Meschkank 2011; Chatterji 2005). Hence the reason one male migrant gave for relocating to Makoko: "I was motivated to relocate to Makoko principally by the success story of my brother who had lived and worked here. . . . I joined him in Makoko at a tender age, and [today] I have become self-reliant, acquiring some basic items befitting the status of a man." A female interviewee also states: "Initially I used to visit Makoko regularly, and I realized that the community is good and comfortable. There is food to eat, things are going well for residents, and there are profitable business opportunities. And so, I was motivated to also migrate here through a friend's connection."

Migration to Makoko follows a chain process. Up to 60.3% of the respondents claimed they were chain-migrated to Makoko by family members (both nuclear and kin), while 39.7% claimed that their migration was facilitated by friends and associates. One interviewee explained: "Since I have found my feet here and in this fishing job like my brother, whenever I visit home, my friends would ask me to show them wealth and request that I took them to Makoko. I usually tell them that survival in Lagos is demanding, but if they are ready to work hard, they can make it, and I am ready to take them to where they can work. I have assisted some of them to come here." Still another interviewee stated: "It was my brother who first came here. I later joined him to be part of his fishing business." When merely viewing the material culture and the social and physical construct of Makoko, an outsider perceives an unwelcoming social structure, entrapped in abject poverty with social and physical factors indicating a "push" out of Makoko for a better life or greener pastures elsewhere. Nevertheless, Makoko residents view the settlement as economically viable.

Makoko is sustained, of course, by a social reality of economic survival and profit making even within its coarse social structure. This social structure welcomes those who are as yet in abject poverty. Makoko thus presents a degree of opportunity for social mobility, even if this is limited to intra-proletarian movement into higher degrees of economic privilege within the slum economy. Hence, migration into Makoko and subsequent reconstruction of the economic capability of the migrant by friends and relatives left behind in the places of departure creates an urge to migrate. The successful migrant assumes the position of the privileged and strategic facilitator of chain migration into Makoko. At this point, the notion of the slum environment as abject and deprived is deconstructed. New discourses and reconstructions of the economic advantages of the slum are evidentially interpreted from the "wealth" of the successful migrant. With notions of work, income, and economic survival, the slum environment at first becomes like a "work environment" for the potential or new migrant. Since the slum thus initially becomes a "work environment," the proletarian worker, who has internalized the discomfort and exploitation of the capitalist environment as normative, views the physical environment of the slum as a mere reflection of the working environment of most peasant work stations. The economic value to be gained from working in the slum, as well as the embedded social capital that comes along with the bonds of unity, friendship, family, and love, become the principal goods derived from the slum environment (Grazian 2009; Annen 2001). This is very different from the elitist construction of poverty, inhuman exposure, crime, disease, and death often recorded in the literature (see for example Shaban 2008; Adelekan 2010; Douglas et al. 2008; Reckner 2002). Consequently, as migrants earn a living, survive, and blossom within the slum, Makoko translates from a "working space" to a "home space"—a place of comfort, to be built, defended, and sustained. This explains the increasingly sprawling nature of the Makoko settlement on the lagoon and the consequent creation of stilt housing commerce and artisanship.

The Social Organization of Stilt Housing

Spatial accommodation (whether residential or for business) is critical for sedentary habitation, survival, and prosperity, irrespective of the location's limitations (Pothukuchi 2003; Culhane 1992). The situation in lagoon Makoko is no different. Every available sheltering space is under a particular unofficial property claim. Respondents thus indicated that access to a housing space is predicated on inheritance (43%), purchase (37.3%), or rent (19.7%). Though it is an illegal slum settlement, lagoon Makoko is also a spatial entity of vibrant property commerce involving peasant property investors, landlords, and tenants. It is thus a center of commercial property exchanges with vested interests and blossoming artisanship trades to provide crucial housing expertise. This being a lagoon community, the dwellings are predominantly erected on ramshackle stilts (Adelekan 2010; Agbola and Agunbiade [2007] 2009). Stilt housing, as well as its associated construction and maintenance expertise, are critical to living and surviving in lagoon Makoko. Data revealed that stilt housing is constructed through hired labor (58.3%), the help of family and friends (28%), and self-construction (11.7%). An interviewee confirms the quantitative finding thus: "We go and buy planks or timber and other building materials from the market, and carpenters and other related workers are the ones we invite to build these stilt houses. . . . Sometimes our friends also help out."

A clear inference from the data above is that the lagoon Makoko slum accommodates a special class of skilled artisans whose special trade in stilt housing construction is critical to the sustenance of Makoko. They possess the critical manpower and skill in identifying high-quality and decay-resistant wood, ensuring firm underwater grounding as the foundation on which they then construct simple but livable stilt houses. Those who cannot afford the services of skilled labor opt for self-construction and/or the help of friends. Here, local knowledge acquired over the years and social capital provide the needed intervention in providing and sustaining shelter. Within the world of the peasant class, lagoon Makoko is thus a "property hub" involving transactional exchanges and rent arrangements between owners and clients. It also has a specialized system of construction and property maintenance involving peasant experts who provide their services on a commercial basis or by social capital.

Challenges and Coping Strategies

Slum environments usually pose enormous survival challenges to residents. These challenges may include economic, political, social, and environmental ones. Of course, residents usually find ways of coping with slum challenges (Aßheuer,

Thiele-Eich, and Braun 2013; Jarrett and Jefferson 2004). The Makoko slum is no different. Respondents identified lack of basic amenities, especially tap water and electricity (90.7%), threat of eviction by the government (100%), and poor living conditions (100%) as challenges to survival in Makoko. Despite these challenges, the respondents affirmed their resolve to remain in Makoko because of the business opportunities in the community (88.3%) and because they just "love it there" (11.7%). This finding is supported by Verma (2012) and Meschkank (2011), whose researches in India confirm the economic vibrancy of the Dharavi slum. In spite of the precariousness of the slum environment, the economic viability of the slum could make it a preferred residence for those who dwell there, very much against the assumptions of outsiders. Furthermore, lagoon Makoko residents cope with municipal challenges by dumping refuse on land (80.3%) and in the lagoon (10.3%), defecating and/or channeling human waste into the lagoon (100%),[6] and treating illnesses by self-medication (herbal medicine, 53.3%, and modern drugs, 18.3%).

Interviewees also confirmed that "till this moment, the major challenge has always been that of eviction by the government. The fear of the unknown is scary and depressing." Yet another interviewee states: "It is the government that is giving us problem, chasing us about, that our children fall into the lagoon and die, some older people develop hypertension and some others are depressed." While the interviewees did not clearly state how they cope with eviction threats, it is important to note that, judging by reports in the media, they cope by appealing to public conscience and to their contacts and/or patrons in political and government circles (Ibiwoye 2014; Okulaja 2013). However, in terms of health and environmental challenges in Makoko slum, the interviewees claimed they coped thus: "There are health facilities[7] on the lagoon. When someone is ill, we take such a person to the clinics on the lagoon or on land. Also, there are herb sellers on the lagoon who prescribe herbal medicine to the sick." Another interviewee states: "We build our stilt houses with toilets . . . and urine and feces are channeled into the lagoon and the currents will sweep them away." Still another interviewee provided further information on sanitation strategy: "We gather and pack our refuse in garbage, and we take it to the land for the LAWMA [Lagos Waste Management Authority] to take it away." Confirming the assertion above, another interviewee explains: "We conduct environmental sanitation[8] on water. . . . We clean the lagoon by removing papers, dirt, and debris, we put them in our canoes and paddle to the shore to drop them into LAWMA vehicles."

Lagoon Makoko remains a precarious environment, challenged with the threat of eviction, lack of basic amenities, poor environmental conditions, and a dearth of modern health facilities. Yet the economic viability of the Makoko environment within the views of the residents makes it a preferred location. Makoko residents thus devise ingenious means of coping with the challenges of survival. The threat of eviction is tackled by "oppressed propaganda" that puts planning authorities and the government on the defensive, especially during election periods. Despite associated environmental pollution, residents discharge human waste into the lagoon due to the lack of sanitation facilities and patronize quack health practitioners and herb sellers for their health needs. Indeed, Makoko is a precarious environment. The peasant residents are, however, able to survive and cope by adapting to the environment, engaging in economic transactions, and minimally maintaining the community through periodic sanitation. They continually swell the population of lagoon Makoko by welcoming new migrants and new births. Of course, the new migrants and births are likewise exposed to the social reality of hardship and precarious survival. They are thereafter socialized into the coping strategies of the community by its more experienced members, who hold it as their duty to sustain the human population at Makoko, lest it go extinct or the official attempts at permanent eviction and demolition succeed.

Conclusion

Makoko slum settlement on the lagoon presents an active agency with a primary objective of ensuring the survival of the slum despite the threats of eviction by the state. Lagoon Makoko appears to outsiders as a poverty-stricken, precarious slum environment, but the embedded social structure instead entails economically active individuals who work in unison with embedded social capital to ensure survival and maintain a critical peasant population whose presence sustains lagoon Makoko's economy and social life. Lagoon Makoko is a peasant-constructed social reality of good life and comfort. The state policy of demolition is politicized and constructed as anti-peasant. Thus, Makoko social structure appeals to public consciousness as a settlement of the "deprived" that deserves support, not eviction. Hence, the successful implementation of government demolition orders is obstructed by public displeasure, likely political backlash and condemnation, and Makoko's active artisanship sector (which quickly rebuilds demolished structures). In the end, lagoon Makoko continues to survive—and expand, with ongoing immigration and new births.

Above and facing page: Makoko lumberers at work. (All photos for this chapter by Adefemi Abdulmojeed Adeyanju.)

Above, Makoko schoolchildren; *below*, petty trade at Makoko; facing page, Makoko waterways.

Above, Makoko transportation; *below*, local snacks vendor.

Part II:
Protest and Struggle
in Latin America

Chapter 4

The Ayotzinapa Massacre

Mexico's Popular Protests and New Landscapes of Indignation

Claudia Delgado Villegas

> *"This really is not a problem: in Mexico whenever a corpse is sought many others are found in the investigation."*
>
> **—José Emelio Pacheco**

The Day of Indignation

On September 26, 2015, the streets of Mexico City roared with thousands of protesters marching to the Zócalo, the city's main square, to meet once again with the parents of the forty-three normalistas of Ayotzinapa who disappeared in the state of Guerrero in 2014.[1] September 26 was declared as "The Day of Indignation." Indignation, because—after a year of what has been publicly condemned as a crime of state and the worst massacre of students in Mexico since 1968—there has been no justice, only 365 days of mass protests demanding two things: that the forty-three normalistas be presented alive, and that those responsible be brought before the law.[2]

A full year has passed without justice. The parents of the forty-three missing students and of the three students killed on September 26, 2014, in Iguala, Guerrero, came back to the Zócalo—the country's symbolic political heart—so that the government could hear them loud and clear: they have not forgiven; they have not forgotten. Those forty-three *are* their children, their boys, the parents said, and they will never give up on them: "We know the government

69

knows where our children *are* . . . hence we mandate them to present our forty-three alive."

"If the government thinks we are stupid, well, today we're here to prove them wrong."

"Here we are, after a year, all of us standing and we're not alone."

"We're not afraid of the government's threats."

"We will give our own lives until we find our children."

A year after the Ayotzinapa massacre, the motto "They were taken alive, we want them back alive!"[3] echoes the logic of the worldwide popular mobilization around the forty-three disappeared students. The basic timeline of what happened on the night of September 26, 2014, has been read, seen, cried, discussed, and written ever since. There are very few in Mexico who do not know the story, or at least part of it, by now. It began when a convoy of normalistas was attacked and later kidnapped in the city of Iguala, about two hundred miles due south of Mexico City. Six people (three normalistas among them) were murdered. Guerrero state police, federal and military forces, and organized crime participated in the attack and the killings. The students were enrolled in the Rural Normal School Raúl Isidro Burgos, located in Ayotzinapa, a town about ninety miles from Iguala. The school is one of seventeen rural normal schools in Mexico.[4] The normalistas were heading to Mexico City to join a demonstration for the forty-seventh anniversary of the student massacre of 1968, which is honored every year in the neighborhood of Tlatelolco.

Hundreds of clandestine graves were found in Guerrero during the first year of deliberately ineffective federal and state investigations around the Ayotzinapa students.[5] The first demonstration for Ayotzinapa took place in Guerrero's capital city, Chilpancingo, three days after the massacre. An escalation of mobilizations, occupations, protests, and demonstrations in over twenty-five states in Mexico and hundreds of cities worldwide came after. A "global action day for Ayotzinapa" was called on the twenty-sixth day of every month for a year.[6] The first demonstration in Mexico City happened on October 8, 2014.

A "National March for Ayotzinapa" was called for November 20 in Mexico City, to coincide with the anniversary of the 1910 Mexican Revolution. The protest marked the peak of the popular mobilizations for Ayotzinapa and thus contributed to defining the second decade of Mexico's twenty-first century as an extraordinary period of social unrest and urban revolt. Protesters turned Mexico City's urban heart into a cityscape of indignation.[7] They took their anger to the streets to occupy and dwell in the urban space. They were a mass of outraged people using over two hundred years of political repertoire drawn from all the major revolts that had ever occurred in the Zócalo: there were impersonations of the priest Miguel Hidalgo y Costilla, who led Mexico to independence in 1810; images of the Virgin of Guadalupe like the ones that accompanied him in the uprising; and banners showing Emiliano Zapata, peasant leader of the Mexican Revolution, or Che Guevara, or political slogans from the 1968 student movement, the Zapatistas of Chiapas (1994), or the peasants of Atenco with their machetes (2001).

In this playful exercise of keeping the talk of the streets alive, protesters found the means to effectively memorialize the nature of the times they are trying to change for future Tlachinollan generations. The most conspicuous examples included banners asking for the resignation of Enrique Peña Nieto from the presidential office—"Peña out!"[8]—and those denouncing the Ayotzinapa massacre as a crime of state—"The state did it!" The megaprotest of November 20 was organized to converge on the Zócalo from different starting points in the city. It moved in three caravans, each of them named for one of the murdered normalistas: Julio César Mondragón, Daniel Solís Gallardo, and Julio César Ramírez Nava. It took several hours for the thousands of protesters to finally reach the Zócalo.

In January 2015, Jesús Murillo Karam, then Mexico's attorney general, aggravated the reasons for revolt when he informed the public that the forty-three normalistas of Ayotzinapa had been executed by the drug cartel United Warriors and their bodies burned in the Cocula municipal waste dump in Guerrero. He doomed himself by adding that these facts constituted the "historical truth": meaning that the investigations and the protests should end, because the case was now closed. The government expected the parents to accept the reality of the death of their sons, period. An "anti-monument" with the number "+43" was built on Avenida Reforma in the seventh month after the massacre.[9] Over 108 people had been detained by then, the majority of them members of the Iguala municipal police.[10] The mayor of Iguala and his wife were arrested in July, becoming the first and only two public servants prosecuted so far. No federal forces or members of the army have ever been charged. On September 6, the so-called Interdisciplinary Group of Independent Experts (known by its acronym in Spanish as GIEI) submitted the "Ayotzinapa Report" to a government tripartite commission: the results of a six-month alternative investigation mandated by the Inter-American Commission on Human Rights, concluding that there was insufficient "scientific evidence" to show that the forty-three students were incinerated in Cocula.[11] With this report, the parents said, the government's "historic lie" was conclusively defeated by the truth.

The Summoning

On September 25, 2015, a day before the megaprotest called for the Day of In-dignation, the parents of the normalistas ended a forty-three-hour hunger strike in the Zócalo: an hour for each of the forty-three missing, every hour represent-ing their tireless struggle.[12] Forty-three seats were placed for the press conference at the end of the collective fasting. The parents arrived at 2:00 p.m. sharp, walk-ing out from the white tents of the small camp a few yards away. Their expres-sions were tired, worn, and humble. Many of them held their eyes downcast, yet they faced the hordes of cameras, reporters, and microphones. "We have hope," they said, backed by a big white banner with the faces of the missing forty-three and the Amnesty International emblem. Words of hope were followed by words of outrage; each of the parents spoke of their own. The day before, the parents had met with Peña Nieto for the second time in a year. Their fury came from that doomed encounter too:

"We got nothing but lies from the president, and abuse from his presidential guards."

"We're angry because this government has done nothing but stab us in the heart."

At the end of the press conference, one of the fathers spoke with me about the meaning of "indignation" and of summoning the outraged from the Zócalo. I recorded his words and later translated them into English:

> For us, "indignation" is a word of respect and rage because we believe that all Mexicans and all human beings have a special place and that all of us are special. And when someone squashes our dignity as human beings, that makes us feel rage and demand that someone respect us; it is mainly a demand of self-respect. That is the meaning of "indignation" for us. We feel full of wrath because this government we have in Mexico believes that Mexicans are fools—that we believe whatever they say. We are angry because they believe we will remain silent, just because they control people through the television. But today we have shown them the dignity of the parents. This has been a year of relentless struggle and I think they will not stop us, despite the threats and all that we have been through this year; we will go on until we eventually find the truth. . . . For us, as the Zócalo is the heart of the city, and the city is the heart of this country in political, economic, and in all terms, we believe that's the reason all eyes, all caring eyes, are looking to this place now, and that is why it is from here that the light of insurgency, the light of the dis-content and protest, will shine on. . . . We hope that all Mexicans who

have shown us their empathy and value each one of us [the parents], and especially those who feel our pain, we hope that they all take to the streets tomorrow, as will the rest of us. And we hope to hear a single cry: the cry for justice, and the presentation of the forty-three alive. But above all, we hope to show that together we are stronger.

43 + 3 + 1

The Day of Indignation was gray and rainy. Once again, the parents marched through the streets of downtown Mexico City carrying 43 + 3 + 1 huge banners: forty-three prints of their missing sons, three for the students murdered in Iguala by police forces on September 26, 2014, and one for the activist Miguel Ángel Jiménez Blanco, who was assassinated in August 2015.[13] The banners carried that day are the dreadful iconic image of Mexico's present state of indignation, a state that (as I will show later on) has turned Mexico City into the city of indignation—a city of the outraged. But the Day of Indignation was also a day for the forty-three parents to share their learning and thank all those who, for an entire year, had not given up but kept assembling in the streets and everywhere else in support of their struggle: the normalistas of Ayotzinapa, unions, social organizations, peasants, students, youngsters, organizers, anarchists, teachers, mothers, fathers, sons and daughters, street vendors, street performers, indigenous people, intellectuals, feminists and women's rights activists, LGBT people, advocates for human rights . . . the list goes on.

The parents thanked those assembled for having journeyed alongside them and asked us not to let them down. The names of the forty-three missing normalistas were read aloud by one of them at the +43 monument, one after another, followed by the chorus "present them alive."[14] After a couple of hours of slow walking—the pace due not to the exhaustion of the parents but to the packed streets—the megaprotest finally entered the Zócalo. This time, the stage for the grim political meeting had no roof and was only large enough to fit the forty-three parents: María de los Ángeles. Rafael and Joaquina. Clemente and Luz María. Antonio and Hilda. Bernardo and Romana. Cornelio and María. Bernabé and Delfina. Margarito and Martina. Celso and Natividad. Francisco and Minerva. Leonel and Gloria. Margarito and Socorro. Damián and Dominga Antonia. Cristina. Ezequiel and Delia. Maximino and Soledad. José Alfredo and María Elena. Yolanda. Epifanio and Blanca. Ciriaco and Bernarda. Genoveva. Oscar and María Araceli. Israel and Ernestina. Nardo and María Isabel. Aristeo and Oli. Luciano and Eudocia. Carmen. Saúl and Nicanora. Santa Cruz and

Abraham. Donato and Metodia. Macedonia. Lorenzo and Beningna. Francisco and Juliana. Joaquina. Eleucadio and Calixta. Estanislao and Margarita. Jaime and Inés. Nicolás and Marbella. Lucina and Juan. Celso and Micaela. Afrodita. Mario César and Hilda.[15]

The ones who spoke and the ones who listened dialogued the rest of that afternoon in the rain. One of the mothers spoke first:

> Again we have shown the government that the people of Mexico are with us and haven't left us alone. The parents are showing that the flame of indignation is still lit, that the flame of our anger is kindling. We have to punish this government because they are not going to do it themselves, and they are the only ones to blame for all that's happening. The night of the twenty-sixth of September and the dawn of the twenty-seventh, the entire police force was involved; they all knew from 5:00 p.m. that the normalistas were going to Iguala. That's why we ask Enrique Peña Nieto to leave, with his whole cabinet. He must return our children alive, so from here I say to him: "Don't be an *hijo de puta*—you know where our children are."

Another mother, an indigenous woman, spoke in her native language and translated her own words into Spanish:

> To all those who raised their voices today, to all who did not stay at home, I say: today the sky is crying, because we have forty-three missing and thousands more. Today the sky weeps because of the missing students. Today I realize that our invitation was not in vain. We were heard. Today you took to the streets; today you walked together to defend our rights. To all those students who walked together with us, I say: this is the time to raise your voices, so that what happened to us does not happen to you, nor to your children or your grandchildren. It's time to raise your voice and change this country. To change this government and not let them continue to rule. It is time now that no country, no indigenous people, should ever let another president take office. It should be every one of you taking the government, not them, not this government with their weapons. We as parents do not carry weapons, yet we are being blocked from passing through. They do not let us protest. As I told the riot police: "Who are you afraid of? Are you afraid of us? Are you afraid of the parents, of the students marching unarmed? Look at you: you have weapons, we don't, and yet you're afraid of us."

Along with these women came the other parents. They spoke their own words, giving their faces, voices, and reasons to the same idea: "Neither the rain, nor the wind, nor the government—no one will stop this movement. We are all Ayotzinapa."[16] Meanwhile the crowd, sheltered by thousands of umbrellas, gave to the parents the cries of justice one of them had asked for the day before:

"No forgiveness, no forgetting, punishment to the murderers!"

"Urgent, urgent, the president must resign!"

"Not with tanks, not with machine guns, Ayotzi will not shut up! Not with tanks, not with machine guns, the people will not shut up! Not with tanks, not with machine guns, Mexico will not shut up!"

"Peña out! Peña out!"[17]

"It is raining rage," read a small piece of blue cardboard attached to a Mexican flag. An older man carried it with his arms raised up. Maybe he was trying to make sure that everybody there, or anyone taking his photograph, could see the message and share it for the times to come. Maybe he was trying to stop the rain: the rain of rage his banner was referring to. Or maybe, like everybody else there, he was just trying to make sense of the student faces shown on those forty-three banners and the faces of the parents carrying them.

A Year of Indignation

The morning of September 26, 2015, Mexican newspapers reviewed the most significant events in an attempt to make sense of the year that had followed the massacre of the normalistas. "Ayotzinapa, an open wound," read a headline in *La Jornada*, one of the major daily newspapers in Mexico.[18] Ayotzinapa occupied the front page along with news on Pope Francis's visit to New York City, including his speech at the 70th General Assembly of the United Nations. The paper's secondary news that day included the release of an official communiqué from the United Nations System in Mexico, ruling in favor of a "general reformulation of the investigation of the events in Iguala" and demanding "to clarify the irregularities [that have] arisen throughout the inquiries such as the use of torture to extract confessions, alteration of evidence, omissions and judicial deficiencies." The day after that, the news reviewed all the major demonstrations demanding justice for Ayotzinapa, including the Day of Indignation and marches, rallies, and vigils in New York, Seattle, Paris, Madrid, Montreal, La Paz, Amsterdam, and Santiago de Chile, among other cities.

Trying to make sense of the major events that shape a country's social history through the lens of news reports can be misleading, but it is worth doing in order to get a sense of the overall state of affairs in Mexico during the year that followed the Ayotzinapa massacre. Newspapers, like photographs, can capture a moment in time. I want to take advantage of this quality to make a brief journey through time and discover a more comprehensive framework for how affairs unfolded and the public responded during the year of indignation that began on September 26, 2014. I want to use it to reflect on the concrete conditions in which people are figuring out the potential of resistance and, ultimately, social change. In the months following the massacre, what did the front pages of *La Jornada* capture?

September 26, 2014. News of executions by the military reached the front page. These were not the executions of Ayotzinapa but of Tlatlaya, in Mexico state—the native state of Peña Nieto. The Mexican army had executed twenty-two people in the town of San Pedro Limón, Tlatlaya. News also referenced student conflict at the Instituto Politécnico Nacional, a major public university. Students were protesting against planned changes in the curriculum and internal regulations. The conflict started in mid-September, when the students declared an indefinite strike and closed down all the university facilities. Student demonstrations shut down the streets of Mexico City several times that fall.

The first news about the massacre of Ayotzinapa appeared a few days afterward, on September 28: "Police shoot normalistas in Iguala: 5 killed," read a headline in the politics section. "Students report 25 injured—one of them brain dead—and an equal number missing." "The body of a young man with signs of torture was found; PGJE [the General Judicial Attorney of the State of Guerrero] counted him as the sixth victim." The same day, the economy section noted that the United Nations Economic Commission for Latin America and the Caribbean had issued a report pointing to the steep decline of wages in Mexico "to its lowest level in 40 years," adding that in Mexican households "six out of 10 members live on less than $10,000 pesos per month"—that is, less than US$600.

November 26, 2014. The minister of the interior announced that for the government of Enrique Peña Nieto "Ayotzinapa is a priority, but we are attending to other conflicts too." By then, news about US concern over Ayotzinapa had reached the front page: "US Senators concerned for the case of the 43." "They urged Obama to offer support in the investigations." So Ayotzinapa was now international news, alongside urban turmoil on the other side of the border: "The National Guard takes control of Ferguson." "More riots across the US." The paper reported protests in New York, Los Angeles, Philadelphia, Chicago, Cleveland, Oakland, Newark, Atlanta, San Francisco, and Minneapolis, condemning a jury's decision not to press charges against the white police officer who had killed Michael Brown on August 9.

January 26, 2015. Ayotzinapa was not much mentioned in the first month of the year, but the news on urban revolt worldwide kept coming. The front page informed of demonstrations against the so-called Public Security Act, promoted by Prime Minister Mariano Rajoy, attempting to amend the right to protest in Spain. In contrast, the streets of Athens were packed with supporters of Alexis Tsipras, leader of Syriza, who had won the Greek legislative elections and declared rejection of the austerity program imposed on Greece by the so-called European troika in exchange for bailout.

In the following months, updates on Ayotzinapa followed national and international concern for the deterioration of human rights in Mexico. There is a "before and after Ayotzinapa," declared the president of the National Human Rights Commission (CNDH) when giving his annual report (March 26, 2015). He described Mexico's present situation as "the worst crisis ever" in terms of arbitrary detentions, forced disappearances, and torture. As the year continued, reports on the economic and social debacle happening in Mexico were as worrying as the ones on Ayotzinapa. "Concessions have 92 million hectares. Canadians dominate with 207 projects; have major deposits of gold. They are followed by US companies, China, Australia, and Japan" (April 26, 2015). A month later, economic news was not any better; headlines were as negative as the previous ones: billions of US dollars were being "injected into the market to stabilize the peso against the dollar." "On Monday, for the very first time, the demand for dollars would not be fulfilled, and the Bank of Mexico placed only $30 million of the $52 million originally scheduled." "The international reserve will keep going down until September 29" (May 26, 2015).

June 26, 2015. The annual US State Department report on human rights that became known in Mexico on this date noted "significant problems" in Mexico, "including the police and the army involvement in serious abuses, comprising extrajudicial killings, torture, forced disappearances and physical abuse." There were additional concerns from civil society organizations like the UN and the CNDH on "poor prison conditions, arrests and arbitrary detentions, threats and violence against human rights activists and journalists, abuse of migrants, domestic violence, trafficking, abuse of disabled persons, discrimination against indigenous [persons], threats against lesbian, gay, bisexual and transgender [persons], and child labor."[19]

August 26, 2015. "Poverty unchanged for 22 years," the paper announced, reporting the conclusions of the National Council for Evaluation of Social Development Policy (CONEVAL) on poverty in Mexico. Data showed the stagnation of family and per capita income from 1992 to 2014. The monthly family income in 1992 was Mex$3,500; in 2014, it was Mex$3,600. By then, the exchange rate was Mex$17.50 to the dollar, and Mexicans, according to data from the central bank, had transferred US$78 billion to bank accounts abroad or to business activities outside the country between January 2013 and June 2015.

September 26, 2015. The circle is complete. The journey through a year of indignation ends here. As mentioned at the beginning of this section, on the morning of September 26, 2015, newspapers included the remarks of Pope Francis at the 70th General Assembly of the United Nations in New York City. Curiously enough, he spoke of dignity, just as the parents of Ayotzinapa did in the Zócalo of Mexico City on the same day. His speech as head of state, making the fundamental connection between dignity and justice, was remarkably coincident with what the parents spoke of: how the Mexican state had trodden on the dignity of an entire people. No human individual or group must be permitted "to bypass the dignity and the rights of other individuals or their social groupings," the pope said. Dignity must be built up and unfolded as a "collective right" and hence a condition that must come from the "limitation of power" by the law itself. Oddly enough, he made these remarks in the same room in which Peña Nieto was sitting at the UN. Peña Nieto had left Mexico in the middle of one of the gravest social crises in the nation's history. He had preferred to ignore it—and yet he had to listen to it after all.

The popular revolt led by the parents of the forty-three missing students has everything to do with this universal sense of dignity. The parents themselves have put it that way. Yet, as I will show in the next section, the nature of this connection has deeper geographical grounds, arising to a great extent from the history of state violence in Guerrero, the home state of the normalistas and one of the poorest states in Mexico.

Welcome to Guerrero[20]

In the year since the massacre, the popular mobilization for Ayotzinapa has resulted in the escalation of state violence in Guerrero via increasing militarization and a new state security plan announced in October 2015. The strategy includes the substitution of federal forces for municipal police in twenty-two of the eighty-one municipalities in the state. The new police are under the command of the Ninth Military Zone.[21] The involvement of both federal forces and the army in the massacre has been a major element in its public condemnation as a crime of state; hence, it is not meaningless to note that with this new plan Peña Nieto is moving the conflict back to square one by bringing the people of Guerrero more of the institutional violence at its origin.

The monopoly of this violence has been recounted many times and by many scholars throughout the twentieth century. The history of grievances is intense, long, and painful, and Ayotzinapa has brought back part of this social memory along with the whole legacy of contemporary popular protest stemming from resistance in the second half of twentieth century. This legacy has given Guerrero nicknames like "Brave Guerrero," "Red Guerrero," or "Red Territory" (Montemayor 1991; Bartra 1996; Illades 2012; González 2015). It reaches back to the militancy of the Mexican Communist Party, the foundation of the Federation of Socialist Peasant Students of Mexico (FECSM), and the opening itself of the Normal School in Ayotzinapa in the 1930s (González Rodríguez 2015; Tlachinollan 2015). These are major left, militant, and populist social institutions that were or still are active in local and regional politics. Lucio Cabañas and Genaro Vázquez are two of the most well-known figures due to their leadership in the peasant guerrilla fighting of the 1960s and 70s.[22] These two emblematic social fighters, as it turns out, graduated from the Normal School in Ayotzinapa. "Maestro Cabañas, the people of Mexico miss you!"[23]

State violence hit the guerrillas in Guerrero hard during the so-called Dirty War in the 1970s and early 80s, a period that joined the annihilation of uprisings in the countryside with the repression of student, activist, and worker insurgency in the city. This was a period of well-documented involvement of government forces in the systematic repression of popular protest throughout the country. In the 1990s, the massacres of Aguas Blancas (the 1995 attack and killing of members of the Peasant Organization of the Southern Sierra by state police forces) and El Charco (in 1998, where a group of students were shot by the army, which alleged they were guerrilla fighters) turned public attention back to Guerrero and its long history of power abuses and impunity. And then again in 2011, the federal police killed two normalistas of the Ayotzinapa School during a peaceful student blockade of the Mexico-Acapulco Highway. The killings occurred under two of the most corrupt and repressive state administrations: the governments of Rubén Figueroa Alcocer (1993–1996) and Ángel Aguirre Rivero (1996–1999), both members of the Institutional Revolutionary Party—the party of Peña Nieto.[24]

Hernández (2014, 124) has analyzed the "political economy of abandonment," arguing that "abandonment" is the language the Guerrerenses use to claim the history of social inequality and dispossession as well as the collective and individual inability to meet people's basic social needs. The language can thus be used to probe the connections among the conditions of poverty, social misery, proletarianization, and the contemporary escalation of migration to the United States, as well as the extent to which these are the result of state actions. The importance of his analysis in the context of the present work lies in the possibility of framing a contemporary geography of abandonment that traces different "rounds of dispossession," carried out through state actions to utterly maintain the long-term class and ethnic inequality of Guerrero, which relegates indigenous peoples to the very bottom of the social hierarchy.[25] The inhabitants of these geographies are, drawing on Hernández's words, people who live on the margins of the state.

The majority of the parents of the forty-three missing students come from within this geography of dispossession: towns like Ayutla de los Libres, Tixtla, Omeapa, Atliaca, Atoyac, Xalpatlahuac, Tecoanapa, Alpuyecancingo de las Montañas, El Pericón, Huajintepec, Arcelia, El Ticui, Juan R. Escudero, Cuatepec, San Cristóbal, Tlatzala, Zumpango del Río, Monte Alegre, Apango, La Montaña, and Malinaltepec. As one of them testified: "The majority of the students of the Ayotzinapa School are poor. Our families are poor, and our only chance was to study in the Normal of Ayotzinapa. . . . We are indigenous. Maybe that's why today they want to get rid of us" (Imprenta de Luz 2014).

Hernández (2014, 147) describes the state of poverty in Guerrero as follows:

> According to the [*sic*] Mexico's Consejo Nacional de Evaluación de la Política de Desarrollo Social, in 2005 Guerrero has the second highest rate of Índice de Rezago Social (Social Gap Index). CONEVAL recognizes three types of poverty in the country: pobreza alimentaria (food poverty); pobreza de capacidades (capability poverty) and pobreza de patrimonio (patrimony poverty). The data for Guerrero (with a total population of 3,115,202) is as follows: food poverty, 40.2%; 50.2%, for capability poverty; and 70.2%, for "patrimony poverty." According to the same source, in 2005 in Guerrero, 19.9% of the population 15 or more years old was illiterate; 7.1% of the population between 6 and 14 years old did not attend school; 58.0% had incomplete basic education; 74.1% had no access to the health care system; 31.6% of the dwellings had soil floors; 29.2% of dwellings lacked toilets; 34.5% had no access to water supply; 8.5% no access to electrical power; and 33.5% of the dwellings had no refrigerator.

In examining the role of the state in producing these local conditions of social vulnerability in Mexico, Robinson (2014) looks to the global scale to consider the role of the US in militarizing Mexico, and he analyzes this strategy as a counterpart to the capitalist globalization of the country. From this perspective, what happened in Ayotzinapa, rather than being considered an accident, must be understood within the context of the broad strategy of militarization that the United States has imposed on the Mexican government in order to protect the transnational corporate interests derived from NAFTA, Plan Mexico, and the Merida Initiative (and now, we might add, the Trans-Pacific Partnership). The United States, he maintains, "is just as much to blame as is the Peña Nieto and previous Mexican regimes for the grotesque crime in Iguala and for the reign of terror against the Mexican poor, the indigenous, and the working class. Plan Mexico has been funded with up to $3 billion from Washington. Steadfast U.S. support for one Mexican regime after another has helped contribute to the absolute impunity enjoyed by those who violate human rights, conduct forced disappearances and massacres, engage in wholesale corruption and violence on a daily basis."

Paired with this large-scale perspective, González (2015) re-creates the contemporary social geography of Guerrero along three major lines: the waves of neoliberal reforms in Mexico,[26] the state of "normalized" (systematic) violence, and the geopolitics around arms trading, drug production, and natural resources (mainly mines and gold).[27] The latter involve US interests—and actual command over large parts of Mexico's national territory. The local picture derived from this analysis describes a state of emergency in Guerrero due to structural violence,[28] within an even larger state of "tolerated extermination" in Mexico due to the nationwide war on drugs: "The forced disappearances perpetrated by criminal groups, the military, the marines, and the police are another consequence of the war on drugs launched by the Mexican government, whose victims [may include anywhere from] . . . 70,000 dead and over 20,000 disappeared, according to the official count, to over 120,000 dead and disappeared, according to independent accounts. This is the grand ossuary the government insists on denying." According to these data, an average of thirteen people have disappeared every day in Mexico since 2012 (González 2015, 51–52).

The Ayotzinapa massacre marks the pinnacle of governmental and social crisis in Mexico after three decades of NAFTA and the neoliberal labor and economic reforms of the administration of Peña Nieto. The technocracy in power is determined to increase poverty and inequality as it wages a war against the indigenous, the poor, and the working class. As we have seen, the state of Guerrero, the second-poorest state in Mexico after Chiapas and the home of the Ayotzinapa Normal School, remains a target of state violence and abandonment. Most of its labor force continues migrating to the United States, and people's ability to meet their basic social needs is being reduced to smithereens, largely due to actions on the part of the state.[29] If any conclusion can be derived from the foregoing analysis, it is the need to go further in examining the long-term connections between state actions and the origins of the Ayotzinapa massacre. Such a task surpasses the objectives of this work for now. Yet, as will be shown in the next and final section, there is another key bond behind this year of indignation and protests that needs to be addressed: the one connecting the mass mobilizations for Ayotzinapa to the rise of urban revolt.

Back to the City

Social crises in Mexico have so far gone hand in hand with a significant rise of *urban* protests. The protests for Ayotzinapa that shut down Mexico City's downtown from the autumn of 2013 to the spring of 2015 are the latest in a series of mass mobilizations across the country. Since the insurrection of the Zapatista Army of National Liberation in 1994, these mobilizations have led many distinct movements for justice to the streets of Mexico City and—more remarkably—to the Zócalo itself. In 1994, the Zapatistas waged war against the Mexican state and were one of the first social movements to denounce neoliberalism as a system intended to annihilate human dignity. In 2001, they ended the "March of Dignity" in the Zócalo after years of sustained, peaceful civil resistance demanding the people's right to land, work, housing, food, health care, education, independence, liberty, justice, and peace. These conditions, they said—and continue saying today—are nothing less than the primary conditions for anyone to live a life with dignity.

The mega-*plantón* (encampment) of 2013, held from May to September by thousands of dissident teachers from the national education workers' union, will remain etched in the urban and social memory of Mexico City. For months, the teachers carried out demonstrations on the streets and occupied the 11 acres of the Zócalo with hundreds of tents, literally building up a city within the city to protest Peña Nieto's education (labor) reforms, which had been approved in February 2013. With time their plantón grew to the point of actually becoming a sort of small town, with basic facilities, inhabitants, and a distinctive urban cultural and social rhythm.

Federal police destroyed the plantón on September 13, in order to have the space clean and ready for the celebrations of Mexico's Independence Day on September 16. On October 5, one of its inhabitants said to me with a great sense of dignity: "Here is a sense of ownership; the government says it is *theirs*. . . . Well, we then also spoke and claimed a sense of ownership, but of people's ownership. [The Zócalo] is *ours*, and the government has no right to take it away from us. When we say the Zócalo is *ours*, we are not saying that it belongs to the teachers, but that this is a place for social protest. That's what we're saying, that is why we have to return this space to the people."

As much as they are echoing the rise of urban revolts all over the world, the social organization and militancy shown in the urban protests of the last two decades—from the Zapatistas to Ayotzinapa—are also indicative of an attempt to consolidate a class-based response to the particular social crisis being experienced in Mexico. On the one hand, an older generation of protesters takes inspiration from a lengthy tradition of hierarchical militancy in unions and urban social movements while a new generation of young urban protesters and social actors exercises more horizontal, multicultural, and self-managed forms of peaceful resistance. On the other hand, the protesters of these two generations have something in common: they are both addressing their call for social justice using strongly class-based language, and they are defending the people's right to use and appropriate public spaces—like streets and squares—for social protest.

Marx and Engels stated in the *Communist Manifesto* that the history of all existing societies is the history of class struggle. This struggle passes through particular spaces and the political use that men and women make of them. All Mexico's major political struggles have gone through the Zócalo, have assembled and rallied in the Zócalo, have spoken of justice from the Zócalo. The right to do so has been gained in the streets. Throughout postrevolutionary Mexico, most of the Mexican proletariat has converged in this space: teachers, electricians, railroad workers, and peasants. In 1938, the country's sovereignty was symbolically defended against American neocolonialism in the Zócalo. On March 23, 1938, workers in Mexico City demonstrated in support of the presidential decree nationalizing the oil reserves. That day, President Cardenas stood on the balcony of the National Palace waving to protesters while a blanket hung on the facade of the Cathedral demanding the end of "capitalist oppression." This was the same oppression that nearly a century before, in 1846, had marched with the firepower of the North American troops through Isabel La Católica Street to hang the American flag in the Zócalo. "To the Zócalo!"[30] was the battle cry of the student demonstrations of July and August 1968, during which—for a moment—a red-and-black flag waved on the flagpole in the main square. The massacre of October 2 came after.

In 2014, the Ayotzinapa massacre once again took the struggle for social justice back to the Zócalo. Guerrero is a state with a strong heart and spirit of resistance, and the persistence and stubbornness of this spirit have contributed greatly to keeping the mobilizations for Ayotzinapa alive. But there is a deep historical connection between Ayotzinapa and Mexico City, and that connection passes through the production of space and its political use for social struggle. From this perspective, the urban protests for Ayotzinapa are as much about mobilizing people for justice as they are a battle for memory and belonging.

As public space, the Zócalo is a physical reflection of the struggle for inclusion in or exclusion from that "imagined community" (Anderson 1983) we call nation: that "illusory community" (Gilly 1997) formed by a superior and an inferior community linked by a relationship of command and obedience. If, in the construction of these imagined or illusory communities, history turns into an instrument for legitimizing the formation and continuation of these ties of command and obedience, then it is worth asking to what extent the urban protests for Ayotzinapa and the concrete ways we are memorializing it are challenging our ideas about this imagined community called Mexico. Whoever has the right to be in the Zócalo has the right to be in the city and hence has the right to be a part of the nation.

Last but not least, the Ayotzinapa massacre has quickened social protests from peaceful to more violent disputes for the public spaces that the local and federal administrations keep privatizing through major commerce, leisure, and consumption projects in the city. The dispute is generating a complex urban landscape of contestation: a cityscape of contestation. On the one hand, the city government struggles to comply with the neoliberal refunctionalization of Mexico City's downtown as they push forward "touristification," "thematization," and gentrification projects, along with securitization and the enforcing of public order. On the other hand, the rise of popular mobilization against police repression and the abuse of state power is turning Mexico City's downtown into a major arena of class struggle. The protests for Ayotzinapa are the continuation of this movement and hence an opportunity to change the city and the way we think about it.

In Mexico City's case, the link between public space and urban protest is in harmony with the Global South's distinctive notions of dignity and justice and hence provides a framework to examine new possibilities and reflect on the meaning of urban revolt. The city itself is becoming what Henri Lefebvre foresaw as a dimension of the possible: a means for spreading and practicing ideas of social justice.

(All photos for this chapter were taken during the demonstrations for Ayotzinapa in Mexico City, 2014–15, by Claudia Delgado Villegas.)

Chapter 5

The Case of the West Zone

Urban Revolt and Social Movement Adaptations in Rio de Janeiro, Brazil

Simone da Silva Ribeiro Gomes

Introduction

To discuss the subject of urban struggles in contemporary Rio de Janeiro is both a theoretical and empirical challenge due to the myriad of problems the city faces in terms of its challenging geography and endemic violence.[1] My main goal in this study is to present some of the findings of my doctoral research on the ongoing political opportunities for militancy in the West Zone of Rio de Janeiro. The research is concentrated in a periphery, which faces several difficulties that will be further analyzed in this text.

When examining a megalopolis like Rio de Janeiro, it is essential to investigate inhabitants living in precarious situations, including local militants who live in vulnerable conditions in communities without adequate services and who face a multitude of violent actors who marginalize them even further. Broadening research on this underworld of urban communities is important to understanding the complex process of mystification that peripheral movements suffer.

Rio de Janeiro is understood, in this research, as a core megalopolis for world geopolitics and for the conflicts and movements that can take place in urban environments, but frequently the specific spaces within the city that generate urban disputes are neglected. As with poor communities in major urban areas across the world, there are local particularities in the social organization and militancy of the inhabitants, and these are the object of this analysis.

Methodology

This study used a qualitative approach that included ethnographic research involving participant observation, with the intention of unveiling some of the potentials and limitations of social movements in an urban periphery. During three years of field observation, nineteen semistructured interviews with young militants between the ages of nineteen and twenty-five were conducted. The militants were active in various organizations, such as popular education groups; cultural movements; LGBT movements; popular anarchist organizations; feminist movements; and antiracist movements, among others.

The diversity of data from the fieldwork must be noted in our case study, as well as the variety of themes the militants worked with. They lived and acted in different neighborhoods in the West Zone, but mainly Campo Grande, Realengo, Santa Cruz, and Bangu.

The data drawn from the interviews demonstrates that the urban militancy they developed had to do with state violence: specifically, fighting against the form of it assumed by the *milícias,*who use violence to control and threaten people living in those areas.[2] A key element was police repression, which happened when militants—individually or collectively—tried to rise up against any injustice. I began my research by frequenting meetings of a popular education group in order to get to know a few local militants, as well as attending events that might attract people identified with issues relating to inequality and economic injustice in Brazil. All interviews were recorded and later transcribed; the names of the militants and their organizations have been altered, as have the specific names of the groups.

The brutality of the conditions they live in and the state's responses to their demands were the main concerns guiding the interviews. The forms of organization amid the urban problems the militants face and the constant menace of violence were unveiled during the interview process. Nonetheless, the solutions the militants proposed for police brutality were very distinct and included cultural and educational solutions intended to enable like-minded people to more freely discuss the problems they daily faced. These tended to avoid any semblance of a mass-scale urban revolt, which would attract negative attention from the state.

I will first introduce some of the contemporary urban struggles going on in Rio de Janeiro, presenting definitions of social movements and of militants and featuring some aspects of their struggles, whether these are more clandestine or able to take place relatively freely. In examining the social organization of urban militancy, I highlight how these movements are silently organized at the margins of society. I then examine the West Zone of the city: its particular confluence of distinct coercive actors, its structural poverty, and the ways in which its challenging geography segregates or facilitates the different struggles that take place there.

Further on, I examine the routine strategies of the militants in the West Zone, focusing on their collective organization in more structured social movements as well as in their quotidian resistance practices. I then conclude with some final remarks on the effects of social struggles in our case study in the West Zone, in highly coercive areas.

Background: Contemporary Urban Struggles in Rio de Janeiro

My main objective in this section is to work on a historical analysis of the urban struggle—mainly, but not exclusively, in relation to community responses to police brutality. To that end, I will briefly present how urban struggles are taking place in the city of Rio de Janeiro, moving on to its idiosyncratic West Zone. I do not intend to be exhaustive, understanding that the full complexity of the urban struggles theme in a megalopolis like Rio de Janeiro extends beyond the scope of this research.

Tilly (2004, 308) defines social movements as repeated public demonstrations in the public space by a large number of people, in defiance of the state and in the name of securing more rights for a given population. Nonetheless, contemporary militancy does not always fit into those twentieth-century definitions, engaging in processes that also take place in virtual platforms, with networks that are transnational and invariably with identity claims, even when it is organized to fight against state violence.

Academic research seldom refers to the members of social movements as "militants" in the sense intended here; words like "militant" and "militia" are commonly associated with more radicalized and possibly terrorist movements. In this paper, however, I understand "militants" as people who take part in a cause and identify themselves with it but do not necessarily constitute a homogeneous population in their own right. While some may engage in social movements, taking part in meetings, sharing tasks, and disseminating their causes both online and in the streets, not all militancy will be institutionalized.

Roberta, from Guaratiba—one of the frontiers of the West Zone, at the outer limit of Rio de Janeiro—is engaged in a popular education group and in hip-hop groups that discuss the right to the city, In her interview, she relates being born in a deprived zone and surviving through the fights she engages in herself. She then states: "*The question is what is to be militant, because I think I was born a militant. I come from a very poor family, and to keep myself alive—to fight to live and like what I do—is not easy: to dance and try to be happy in a city that imposes a lot of things. I think to militate is to be resistant and have that strength, and I think poor people are in that place, so I was born with it. I think militancy is to be in a space of trying to live, not just survive.*"

It is, however, important to consider even local urban militancy as part of a transnational framework, since—both in terms of claims they make and networks they establish, mainly by virtual communication—the local movements communicate with movements that share their causes, however geographically distant.

On transnational activism Tarrow (2005) states that, although the claims made by militants may be transnational, the resources are drawn from personal networks, and the opportunities are accessed through the local communities in which they live. Perhaps the most interesting characteristic of this form of activism is how militants connect the local and the global. The phenomenon of acting collectively requires activists to marshal resources, become aware of opportunities, and frame their demands in ways that enable them to join with others. Across borders the difficulties are greater, especially because in deprived contexts such as the West Zone of Rio de Janeiro, the security risks are more substantial while financial resources are less, so actions must be based on economic considerations and well planned.

The case of Rio de Janeiro, known for its historical struggles and for being the main landscape of the Brazilian military dictatorship (which lasted twenty-one years, from 1964 to 1985), helps explain the demobilization of social movements presently. The highly repressive environment during that time—especially the persecution, torture, and incarceration of militants, which severely inhibited social action in the following years (Loveman 1998; Gomes 2015)—has had lasting effects on urban movements, resulting in the picture described by the popular education militant Roberta: "*I think all movements in Rio are disarticulated, so the escalator is going down and we're trying to go up. It's an effort; it's not just a force that you can generate by yourself.*"

The disarticulation takes place in a context of severe cases of state violence. That said, in spite of the repressive environment, Rio de Janeiro currently has many important movements. For example, the struggle for housing is one of the most important battlefields in a city dealing with a wave of expropriations and other abuses by public officials in the wake of the World Cup in 2014 and the

Olympics in 2016. In that sense, the struggle of Vila Autódromo, a deprived zone in a wealthy part of the West Zone, became famous for its popular mobilizations, as well as for the militants from other parts of the city who came to join in that important movement against mass eviction.

Within a tense political climate, the movement arose as a symbolic critique of the Olympic project and the way it is currently being utilized to justify removals all over the city, creating a commission that, together with specialists, proposed the "Vila Autódromo People's Plan." The movement fights repression by the state in its many attempts to forcibly remove people from their houses.

Another important struggle of regional and global importance shares a cultural perspective: feminist and antiracist movements in Rio de Janeiro have also become increasingly significant. Feminist movements lead many marches that gather militants in different parts of the city, as well as leading small and university groups to discuss feminism. The annual Marcha das Vadias is an essential gathering for movements and militants all over the city.[3]

Antiracist movements are also very important in Brazil, as it was the last country in the Western world to abolish slavery, in 1888. In Brazil, half the population is Black, and Rio de Janeiro was one of the main ports for the slave trade in former centuries. It is notably one of the cities whose Black population exceeds its Caucasian and mestizo populations and where there are major battles against both institutional and personal racism. From racially homogenous groups like Coletivo Denegrir, which is based at a public university, to thoroughly heterogenous ones, the historical struggle has an identity component that easily blends with Rio de Janeiro's history.

Another social movement expression is the great number of active popular education groups in some parts of the city, especially in favelas in the city center. Such groups have also gained ground in the North and West Zones, with a strong component of awareness raising and the declared objective of enabling students to access public universities. These groups gather militants from a range of movements that are actively engaged in getting poor students to access higher and free education. They draw on Paulo Freire's concepts of pedagogy of the oppressed in a struggle for the democratization of knowledge.

Lastly, but without claiming to have comprehensively presented all the movements people engage in, I would like to note another important and idiosyncratic movement in the city of Rio de Janeiro: the Favelas movement, which seeks to strengthen the rights of people who live in precarious settlements. Young people seem to be the majority in this movement's acts, marches, and meetings to discuss mainly state violations to the rights of *favelados* (a generic term for people who live in areas featuring difficult terrain, which are violent due to high levels of poverty, drug trafficking, and police violence). The Forum de Lutas de Manguinhos and Coletivo Papo Reto are important related favela movements.

All these movements share a common struggle against violence, which in the case of Rio de Janeiro has to do necessarily with police violence. The military police of Brazil, an anachronistic institution established in 1808 to protect the Portuguese nobility established in Rio, is one of the few police corps that remains subsumed to military law while being dedicated to petty crimes and regular policing of the streets. The result is that policemen trained for war walk the streets of the favelas and the city's peripheries, not uncommonly acting with brutality and killing one out of every two thousand people every year, all over the country.

In this sense, Della Porta and Tarrow (2005) stated that the makers of demands are not the only ones who rely on common repertoires: authorities also share a repertoire of repressive tactics. The same police known for incurring high death rates are the ones policing protests and social movements with the same repressive repertoire used during the antiglobalization protests in Seattle: strong shows of force, closures of streets where demonstrators intend to march, mass arrests, rubber bullets, and pepper spray.[4]

The West Zone: Militias, Poverty, and Resistance

Our case in the present study does not take place in just any part of Rio de Janeiro's complex web of problems and organizations of resistance but in an area that is one of its most intricate, due to violence rates, poverty, public transportation problems, and other issues, especially those that are drug related. The West Zone of the city can be divided into a densely populated wealthy area and the poorer area that I have chosen to analyze. The latter includes neighborhoods outlined and populated by the train line opened in the twentieth century, such as Campo Grande, Santa Cruz, Realengo, Bangu, Barra de Guaratiba, Cosmos, Deodoro, Gericinó, Guaratiba, Inhoaíba, Sulacap, Magalhães Bastos, Paciência, Padre Miguel, Pedra de Guaratiba, Santíssimo and Senador Camará.

As one interviewee put it: "*The West Zone here, from Magalhães Bastos to Santa Cruz, is very interesting, very rich, and has changed and suffered a lot. And all those things . . . the UPP and the widespread violence—the West Zone is a big reflection of all that.[5] It's like we're living today in a state of siege*" (Diogo, antiracist movement, Santa Cruz). After all, we are talking about an area with the lowest human development rate in the city of Rio de Janeiro, amid high social inequalities and daily realities that stand in stark contrast to richer areas of the city.

Among other factors, what draws those highly populated areas together are the high rates of poverty, the distance from the city center and its jobs and cultural equipage, and the strong presence of the criminal groups known as milícias. First, there is a shared perception that both in peripheral areas of Rio de Janeiro and in favelas, the Brazilian state has failed to exercise an effective monopoly on the means of organized violence (Pinheiro 1997). Corrupt police strengthen drug traffickers by taking bribes that allow the traffickers to operate openly in the favelas and peripheries, as is the case in the West Zone (Pessoa 2002; Leeds 1996), taking advantage of the considerable distance from the media and public opinion.

The conditions of violence in those areas are diverse, but it is important to note that they have to do with not only drug trafficking but also the corrupt police force and its more sadistic variant, the milícias. The latter groups are made up of armed agents of the state (plumbers and police officers) and former agents, such as retired military, who alongside traffickers control entire regions. Their offer is protection, and for that they charge traders and inhabitants weekly or monthly, as well as monopolizing several economic activities in those neighborhoods, like gas, alternative transport, and cable TV.

The clientelist functioning of those criminal groups includes not only traffickers but also state agents, a new type of political actor linked to a wider privatization of violence, whose political position in poor communities stems from an appropriation of state power made possible only by the unique ways international illegal markets have expanded into Rio de Janeiro. The new forms of clientelism developed by these newly empowered criminal enterprises involve the deployment of an illegal network that brings criminals together with state and social actors to engage in a variety of activities (Arias 2006).

Those enterprises gained public attention in 2008 in Rio de Janeiro, according to Cano and Duarte (2012), especially for the torture and death of a journalist investigating the phenomenon of milícias. The violent milícias are mostly located in the West Zone of Rio, in Campo Grande and Santa Cruz, both around 40 miles from the city center. Campo Grande accounts for most of the complaints about the activities of *milicianos* made by inhabitants to a confidential state hotline, leading the area with more than 15% (followed by Santa Cruz, with 7%).

The historical coercion of the milícias, mainly acting in those remote areas of Rio de Janeiro, can be compared to an irregular enterprise of private security, with the addition of profits from the monopolies from which they gain most of their funds. The continuum of fear in which they operate unveils the lack of security in which those who inhabit the poor and distant zones of Rio de Janeiro live;

most are too intimidated to denounce any criminal or illegal conduct. Moreover, the fact that many of those criminals are agents of the state means they know how the state apparatus works and how the investigations might be carried out. This allows them to interfere. Their networks include politicians at both the municipal and federal levels, which makes them even more difficult to prosecute.

So the persistent violence facing contemporary Rio de Janeiro does not reflect an absence or collapse of state power but a particular articulation of state, social, and criminal relations, where state power is highly mixed with the service of criminal interests (Arias 2006). What the situation also reveals is a status quo of draconian state violence that nevertheless fails to control drug-trafficking violence in Rio de Janeiro, especially in its most deprived areas like favelas and peripheries. This has the paradoxical effect of reinforcing criminal legitimacy, as residents suffer police abuse and lose faith in the state. Among the difficulties faced by the inhabitants are, according to Zaluar (1998), that drug traffickers maintain prominent roles in most poor communities and their conflicts with police are continuous.

But it was not only traffickers who pointed to coercion forces, especially clientelist ones, as being equally or more frightening. As Roberta states, "*It's a big issue in Guaratiba, where there are many farms and rural areas owned by powerful people. So these spaces, including many slaughterhouses, are places to dump the bodies. There are still many cases of cronyism, of people knocking on your door and telling you 'I'm the owner of that farm there and I want to widen the space, and your house is so near that I need you to get out.' And you don't have another option, you have to leave your house, because you're afraid to die, and there's a possibility, though not a certainty, that this guy will kill you. So you feel vulnerable, you don't know the mechanisms to fight against that, you feel the absence of the state to support you.*"

The existence of external social forces and organizations that not only resist efforts to extend the rule of law but also engage with state actors to promote illegal activities and rights violations (Arias 2006) is an important factor to consider with respect to the coercion that takes place in the regions we studied. Nonetheless, the fear is so widespread that one cannot necessarily decipher what it is that actually frightens them. As one militant puts it: "*Walking through certain spaces can be dangerous, especially at night. I know there are places that are dangerous because people say they are and others where you can't walk, where lighting is precarious. You don't see armed people all the time, but you know that you can be raped or robbed; it's other [forms of] violence. I've recently stopped walking around my own neighborhood*" (Carina, popular education movement, Santíssimo).

What is most interesting for the purposes of the present study is how social movements in highly coercive zones manage to resist, and what strategies the militants in those regions use to survive and maintain their struggles. In a context of ongoing violence, existing theories of democratization have succeeded in building a model for how social networks can help translate protest into concrete political change when traditional strategies for political transformation are ineffectual. Nevertheless, this is not enough, since extremely violent communities are much harder for militants to be successful in. This includes, in particular, dictatorships wherein movements become targets of government repression on a regular basis (Arias 2004).

The risk those militants run is becoming the targets of corrupt officials or criminals (Leeds 1996). Authors such as Arias (2004) aim to explain the local-level political organizing of social movements in those areas by using the model of networks, which would transcend conventional understandings of state-society relations by allowing participation from nontraditional political actors such as international organizations and the media. This model explains how social groups can remain active even under the threat of violence. Being horizontal organizations, they also work based on connections among actors with similar interests and by exploiting the skills of different member groups in order to obtain political gains.

Arias (2004) argues that, through a network, groups with similar objectives can share work and risk among themselves. The networks help member groups accomplish complex objectives under difficult circumstances by allowing those that are subjected to violent conditions where they live to be exposed to risks in a way that promotes change. If the militancy is organized in local-level networks, that raises the cost to violent actors of silencing individual groups.

On the functioning of militancy networks, Roberta tells us: "*I've taught break dance since [I was] very young, so I ended up identifying with the people leading this popular education project, as well as with their socialist group, and I ended up in several networks . . . [including] a network with lots of popular educators. . . . We never know, we can't actually tell the extent of what we're getting ourselves into from the inside.*"

Finally, one must take into account the June 2013 protests, Brazil's biggest national protest wave in two decades, whose immediate trigger was an increase in public transportation fares, although the list of grievances quickly expanded to the precarious state of public infrastructure and services, public spending on the World Cup and the Olympics, corruption, and urban violence. Here this emblematic situation becomes analytically more complex (Alonso and Mische 2015). The protest wave in 2013 was representative of the type of mobilization that is possible in the city center, as well as of how coercive agents react in more distant zones.

A young militant affirms that a march in late 2013 was paradoxically initiated by the milicianos themselves. The militants only found out a few hours after it started, with the support of local politicians who shouted, "*It's no use coming masked—we will discover who you are and you'll suffer the consequences.*" The interviewee continues: "*After that, the march had around three hundred students—do you have any idea of how hard it is to get three hundred students in a march in Campo Grande?—we saw two militants of our group speaking with the guys that had the microphone there, but we had to run after that, not only from the regular repression—this time they were heavily armed*" (Pedro, popular education movement).

Militants' Routine: Strategies in a Highly Coercive Area

This section will seek to further explain how social movements in highly coercive areas structure their actions. The West Zone of Rio de Janeiro will serve as a test case for the hypothesis that high rates of violence and selective repression severely discourage social movements from acting and force actions to be clandestine, avoiding urban revolts. I will mention some of the resistance techniques I observed from the reports of the militants interviewed, but first I will try to lay a theoretical groundwork for understanding what can be done in such violent neighborhoods.

With no intention of being geographically determinist, it must nonetheless be noted that spatial structures such as the built environment, communications infrastructures, and transportation, as well as the configuration of mountain ranges and rivers, set real constraints on social actions. Yet even those extremely solid and durable challenges can be enabling for social movements (Sewell 2011). River valleys and mountain ranges might constrain communication, but this spatial constraint is also an advantage to those who are positioned to serve as agents of communication between adjacent valleys.

Additionally, the relative isolation of mountain geography, with locals having specialized knowledge of the terrain, enhances the chances of militants becoming involved in highly subversive activities, as with the example of guerrilla militants. The West Zone of Rio de Janeiro is surrounded by a mountainous area known as Maciço da Pedra Branca, with a recent history of military maneuvers taking place in the highlands after several confrontations in the 1980s.

If one observes the distance of this region from the city center, as well as the limited entrances to its neighborhoods, which are carefully watched by people who work with the local milícias, one understands the necessity of limiting social action to a certain space. What contentious politics do, after all, is attempt to overcome deeply rooted structural disadvantages. This is the case if one takes into account a spatial agency that may convert disadvantages into advantages when activists enact certain practices and countermeanings in their involvement. The restructuring of those meanings can show a strategic valence of space in new spatial structures and relations (Sewell 2001). Militants produce space by changing the meanings and strategic uses of their environments.

In Rio's violent context, militants are confined to "everyday forms of resistance," in the terms introduced by Scott (1985, 1986) and Joseph (1990). For those thinking about a continuum of peasant resistance, it is important to note that it may proceed without overt protest and with little or no organization; such "routine" resistance has historically lain at the core of peasant politics. What Scott (1990) calls analysis of the "everyday forms of peasant resistance" can contribute valuable insights to a broader conceptualization of Latin American banditry, a category in which we place the main criminal actors, including the police and politicians, in Rio de Janeiro.

Peasant resistance, as conceptualized by Scott (1985, 1987), makes no requirement that resistance take the form of collective action, let alone overt protest. His definition includes "any act by a peasant (or peasants) that is intended either to mitigate or deny claims (e.g., rents, taxes, corvée, deference) made on that class by superordinate classes (e.g., landlords, the state, moneylenders) or to advance peasant claims (e.g., work, charity, respect) vis-à-vis these superordinate classes" (Joseph 1987, 419). This resistance, even if entirely unanticipated and long-lasting, does not need to take the form of collective action. There is also symbolic resistance, which is critical.

Scott seeks to build a definition of collective action rooted in what he considers peasant resistance that has always proceeded on a day-to-day basis, outside the bounds of strictly organized movements—and I agree, based on my research. What Scott calls everyday forms of resistance are daily strategies used by relatively powerless groups, among which we can highlight sabotage, theft, false compliance, slander, and other daily practices.

The most important trait shared by those strategies is that they represent a way for peasants to help themselves that usually avoids a direct and likely costly confrontation with elites (including organized crime). One important feature that we observed as quintessential for the militancy in the West Zone is that the peasants typically avoid any direct symbolic confrontation with authorities or with armed groups, operating within a framework that requires a regular state of anonymity. As Scott says: "There is rarely any dramatic confrontation, any movement that is particularly newsworthy. . . . It is seldom that the perpetrators seek to call attention to themselves. Their safety lies in anonymity" (1987, 422). As Junior, an anarchist from Realengo, puts it: "*What I think is essential is anonymity. Those who get here and start showing off won't last for long. [Those who succeed are] people who come here and face their work as only work, and do not intend to run for anything in the congress or other public office in a few years. I mean, anonymity is the key, as is the work you do on a daily basis. Instead of doing big events, trying to sit with five people and do it routinely is much more important.*"

What Scott tells us about the peasantry is also valid for militants in violent zones. They have been less concerned with formal changes in the arrangements governing the overall state of affairs but still focus on attempts to mitigate the most harmful effects of those arrangements, which impact their lives.

The strong and pragmatic goal of the daily resistance, as discussed by Scott and later Joseph (1990), is not to overthrow or immediately transform the ruling system but rather to survive daily. This form of peasant organization can be expanded to militants in violent areas, who are often isolated from outside allies and have historically confronted formidable obstacles to mobilization. They are to a significant extent unable to organize collective action.

After all, as is the case with the wide range of resistance by peasants in Malaysia surrounding which Scott (1987) developed his theory, not all movements involve contentious politics and direct action. A highly restrictive definition of social movements does not, as Joseph (1990) argued, include the everyday forms of peasant resistance, and that is reductive, though of course we must maintain distinct categories for forms of resistance such as social movements and prepolitical activities, which may enable a better understanding of how the system of domination in which they occur functions. We cannot reduce the open, radical political activity of the subordinated to sporadic acts of resistance, either—but we must nevertheless avoid letting the structures of domination define for us what is and what is not a popular movement.

First let us consider how distance from the center of a megalopolis like Rio de Janeiro affects local militants. Ana, a feminist, reported on the First Encounter of Women of the West Zone in Campo Grande, 2013: "*Political acts, such as marches and other things, always take place in the South Zone and in the center of the city; we must bring them here* [into the peripheral areas where we live]."

The feminist militants of more outlying zones must also consider other forms of oppression related not only to machismo but to its consequences when moving around town: "*People who live here in the West Zone know the difficulties of mobilizing here. The gender issue is always important to us. . . . Women who regularly commute to and from the city center know the problems and dangers of coming back at night after a certain hour"* (Clara, feminist, on the First Encounter of Women of the West Zone, Campo Grande, 2013).

Young feminists articulate a strategy that is very important for militants who suffer from veiled threats, which is to forget about the fear they might experience. They may have to suppress their feelings entirely. Amanda, a militant feminist of Pedra de Guaratiba, affirms, "*I have noticed that it is necessary to lose fear. I'm tired of waiting for the next day's bus in the city center to go back home. A friend of mine and I, she lives in Camará, we go out by ourselves to the marches and go back by ourselves, and yes, we do it, we make the conscious effort of letting the fear go.*"

Another commonly used strategy that was widely mentioned by interviewees was blatant lying and dissimulation about the nature of their activities. According to Scott (2011) in his investigation on subordinated groups in Malaysia, political life under severe repression must incorporate disguise, lies, and evasive behavior, while at the same time keeping a straight face and an enthusiastic attitude.

The creation of safe places for militants is also a quintessential part of surviving in contexts like these. The strategy of having a central hub, even if established somewhat accidentally, which must be very careful not to attract the attention of repressive forces, deserves to be noted. A popular education group in Campo Grande, functioning in a house where other meetings also take place, performs this role of meeting point, where militants (as well as those who look to the militants as people who might know what to do in a context of rights violations) can come for advice.

According to Scott (2011), such spaces must be understood as belonging to the quotidian forms of resistance, being enclosed social spaces where resistance feeds itself and becomes meaningful. Such places do not demand coded speech. They are places where people need not fear the consequences of their combative actions and where, beyond the reach of oppressive relationships, they can talk freely. Nonetheless, this territory must be rather isolated, so that no control, vigilance, or repression reaches people who share similar experiences of domination. Roberta, a popular educator, tells us:

> Everyone is trying to understand this [June 2013] movement, and to that end people found in our group a focal point of resistance in which to exist and think together—not to find answers, because nobody had those, but to give a hug, cry together—people found in our house that place. We did not hold a meeting, but thirty people spontaneously showed up in the house anyway, so we got a bit overwhelmed and frightened because we lost the dimension of it, of how we became a hub, and we felt pride but also fear. And if we're a hub for the people, how long

can we maintain ourselves in this house? Because the milícia always ends up knowing what we're doing there, and if they're not happy with that, they can do anything they want with the space and with us.

All these strategies take place in environments with constant displays of force. Thais, a popular education militant, confirms this: "*When the milicianos are around I don't feel safe. At night they're everywhere, going around the place; every Saturday they charge me a fee for the establishment I work in. At 8:00 p.m. they're already in the streets, armed, especially on weekends. Every Thursday they have a ball showing off their guns. It's completely unsafe.*"

For Scott (1985), those public displays of force must be counterpoised by resistance acts, since resistance relations are also integrally linked to power relations, which produce frictions by using the same power to extract services and taxes from the dominated, against their will. This power is exercised not only by the official authorities in the West Zone but also by milícias and corrupt policemen on a daily basis, through public shows of force, public punishment, and other subterfuges.

Final Remarks

Resistance can be observed even in highly coercive environments. However, the resistance in the West Zone does not necessarily take the traditional form of social movements militating explicitly against the causes of oppression. Regulatory regimes and government policies influence the forms of struggle and repression in a way that makes militants more aware of the dangers they face, and for that reason they organize themselves beyond the boundaries of constitutional or legal constructs. Under such conditions, the urban revolt must be clandestine.

It was not my intention to present an exhaustive picture of the urban struggles in Rio de Janeiro but rather to shed light on some lessons that can be learned from this case study in the poor peripheries of the West Zone. The first of these is that the struggle might be organized in an underground network trying not to call attention to itself, existing in a state of anonymity that goes unnoticed by people looking for signs of traditional social movement organization. A quotidian resistance is also part of this struggle, made up of the everyday acts that try to undermine coercion at its fringes, with tactics such as lying and dissimulating about struggle activities and finding a safe place to encounter each other.

Even if, at first glance, these small and of necessity unnoticed acts of militancy might not seem revolutionary, one must not neglect the transformative potential of quotidian urban struggles. What this case study aimed to address was the extent to which resistance can operate beyond the boundaries of legal constructs and the degree to which it can be successful in spite of coercive forces. The organization of militants in the West Zone of Rio de Janeiro, together and separately, in their quotidian sabotage, is, one might affirm, a form of mitigation of the effects of neoliberalism and the privatization of security. The different groups these militants represent and the performative politics they engage in constitute a politics of silence: ever aware of the need not to call attention to itself, yet addressing crucial problems of public security through cultural activities.

Chapter 6

The Uruguayan Recyclers' Union

Clasificadores, Circulation, and the Challenge
of Mobile Labor Organization

Patrick O'Hare

This chapter focuses on the importance of circulation to the organizing
of Uruguayan waste pickers and informal-sector labor more generally.
Research is based on ethnographic fieldwork conducted in 2009–2010
and 2014–2015 with the Uruguayan waste pickers' trade union, the Unión de
Clasificadores de Residuos Urbanos Sólidos (UCRUS). *Clasificadores* is the name
given in Uruguay to these workers who are dedicated to recovering recyclable
materials (principally cardboard, paper, plastics, and metal). They work either
in the streets (with bicycles, carts, or horses and carts); at the municipal landfill;
or in cooperatives and at municipal plants. There are estimated to be between
three and nine thousand clasificadores in Montevideo alone, and the group is
widely considered to be the most exploited link in the national recycling chain.[1]
Their low incomes, lack of social security, and exposure to environmental risk
are seen as subsidizing the profits of the formal recycling sector (Elizalde et al.
2012). Given these circumstances, I set out to explore the distinguishing features of the trade union's organization within the Uruguayan informal recycling
sector. In the absence of key traditional union tactics such as striking, how did
the UCRUS attempt to pressure or leverage its antagonists? How did it attempt

to organize such a dispersed sector, and which of its constituency's issues did it have to mediate?

The intensified circulation of persons, commodities, and ideas has been recognized as a key characteristic of the globalization of capital and the information revolution (Castells 2000, 502). It is my purpose here to look at the centrality of circulation from below, among those reacting to deindustrialization, fluctuating commodities markets, and workforce dispersal. As Lee and LiPuma (2001) note, a focus on circulation is hardly new within anthropology. British social anthropology was arguably born with Malinowski's 1922 study of Trobriand Islanders and the circulation of shell bracelets and necklaces in the Kula ring trade network; Levi-Strauss (1969) applied linguistic models to the circulation and exchange of precapitalist societies; and Appadurai (1986) and Kopytoff (1986) turned to the question of value in the social life, circulation, and biographies of things and commodities. If anthropology's history is bound up with the study of circulation, the discipline also played an important role in the theorization of the informal sector; indeed, it was anthropologist Keith Hart (1971) who coined the term in his doctoral study of male labor activity in Accra. Researching the organization of workers in the informal sector is increasingly relevant as the ratio of informal to formal workers continues to grow, challenging previous assumptions that informal-sector workers will eventually be incorporated into the formal sector (Gallin 2001).

Rather than aiming at a theorization of the materiality of circulation or its effects as a performative metaphor, as in recent anthropological approaches (Lee and LiPuma 2001; Carsten 2013), this chapter sticks close to ethnographic description, since its purpose is to engage not so much in disciplinary analytics as in researching and indeed aiding the organization of informal-sector workers (Atzeni 2014). In an important way, circulation for clasificadores and their union involves fighting for the *right* to circulate in the city, and their case thus connects with a renewed interest in various "rights to the city" (Lefebvre 1968; Harvey 2008, 2012). Beyond circulation, this chapter speaks to other challenges for unions attempting to organize in the informal sector, such as the lack of an immediate employer; the representation of informal and formal workers in the same trade sector; and demands that may be related to rights and "spatial" issues rather than pay claims. Rather than constituting an example of a fight to *receive* a service (such as electricity, water, and so on), the clasificadores' struggle includes the demand to be able to *provide* one in the face of state attempts at regulation, formalization, and dispossession.

The first section of the chapter offers a brief history of the UCRUS, highlighting how the regional circulation of recycling activists shaped its program and

ideas, and how circulation and blockage played a key role in its two most important events. I then turn to circulation as a demand that is also enacted performa-
tively as a tactic. The following section looks at efforts to restrict the circulation of
recycling workers who navigate by horse and cart (*carreros*) in the city by sedenta-
rizing them into recycling plants, and the ways in which the UCRUS had to mediate the circulation of waste materials between different groups of clasificadores.
Finally, the chapter turns to the demands placed on UCRUS activists to circulate throughout the city, comparing this "mobile unionism" with the "sedentary
unionism" of the trade union congress Plenario Intersindical de Trabajadores–
Convención Nacional de Trabajadores (PIT-CNT). The conclusion attempts to
draw together these different examples of circulation and suggests the relevance of
the case of the UCRUS to research on the "unconventional" labor movement and
the struggles of the global poor and working classes.

UCRUS: A Short History

According to the PIT-CNT delegate who coordinated with clasificadores, the
UCRUS was a "very peculiar" union. It did not deal with a direct employer but
rather made its claims to public bodies, the Intendencia (municipal government)
in particular. Clasificadores were not municipal employees, however, and thus
lacked a range of tactics available to public workers, not least the withdrawal of
their labor. Aside from this, the clasificador labor force was precarious, dispersed,
and fluctuating, with many clasificadores coming in and out of the activity as
they obtained short-term odd jobs. The clasificador was, for the delegate, something of an abstract entity, with its shifting population comparable to those of
seasonal industries like fishing or farm work. Yet despite the peculiarities of the
sector, the UCRUS boasted being the only recyclers' organization anywhere in
the world to be affiliated to a national trade-union federation.

The history of the collective organizing of Uruguayan clasificadores can
mostly be divided into two interrelated areas: the formation of cooperatives and
the development of the trade union. With regard to the cooperative movement,
one early example of this was the Redota cooperative in the working-class La Teja
area of Montevideo in the 1990s, which failed to gain support from the PIT-
CNT. In the 1970s, clasificadores focusing on the paper trade had been subject to
severe police repression in the Ciudad Vieja (the city's old town). Not only were
their carts burned and horses confiscated but they were also evicted from central
urban spaces where they were either living or collecting their materials. An in-
dication of some form of organization among these workers was that they sent

a delegation to the Intendencia to protest the importance of their activity to the economy, as the newspaper *El Día* reported on September 17, 1974. In the late 1990s, a clasificador of the older generation who had once been victimized by the dictatorship attempted to organize clasificadores into a union, with limited success. Another key predecessor of the formation of UCRUS was the Organización San Vicente, a territory-based advocacy group linked to the radical priest Padre Cacho that helped make clasificadores visible and still fights for improvements in their treatment, sanitation, and living conditions.[2] There have been other moments of intense repression reported in the press, but organized resistance or opposition from clasificadores is usually not documented there, though it may well have occurred.

As for the UCRUS, its story is intertwined with that of a figure whom I will call El Abuelo ("The Grandfather"), its longtime advisor and cofounder. A former fisherman and political militant, he had begun working with a group of carreros, promoting their cooperation so that they might achieve better prices selling their materials collectively. They held their foundational assembly in April 2002 and were able to send a delegation to May Day for the first time that year. The union was strengthened when the incipient group was contacted by clasificadores at the Felipe Cardoso landfill toward the end of 2002. The landfill had long attracted the largest concentration of clasificadores in the city, and these often had to defend themselves against the violence of police stationed there. In 2002, they were prohibited from accessing waste materials, and a group of clasificadores decided to chain themselves across the road from the entrance. El Abuelo and others arrived and suggested that they cross to the gate itself to prevent the entry of municipal trucks. This confluence at the dump of clasificadores from the landfill with El Abuelo and the carreros with whom he had been working is the most important foundational myth of the UCRUS. El Abuelo described it this way: "We didn't say, 'Cross [the street],' we told them, 'Let's cross.' Because it's predictable that the police won't like it. And that we'll have problems. Let's cross and take whatever the risks are. But we understand that it's the only way. Two hours later, word came from the Palacio [Palacio Legislativo, the city legislature]: 'We'll negotiate.' So, [it was] a triumph . . . as you can imagine, an exceptional triumph."

In a vulgar application of the literature on the metabolism of the city (Wolman 1965; Newman 1999; Heynen, Kaika, and Swyngedouw 2006), blocking access to the dump effectively meant shutting off the city-subject's only toilet, refusing to let it relieve itself.[3] Negotiations were successful and clasificadores were granted access to an internal road that lay in between two dumps. There, thirty trucks specially selected for the quality of their material would be dumped and shared by around 150 clasificadores, an improvement on the previous arrangement. This marked, in the words of El Abuelo, the founding (or refounding) of the UCRUS, and it was an event to which he referred back to frequently, if not excessively. (Uruguayans are said to be particularly nostalgic, and one militant spoke of El Abuelo's thinking back constantly to this event as "maracanando"— obsessively reminiscing as the nation did over its victory in the 1950 World Cup at Maracanã Stadium, Brazil). After a period of several years, the workers at the landfill were moved to an improved site. In their first steps toward cooperativization, they adopted the provisional name Cooperativa El Abuelo in honor of the man who helped them win that crucial first struggle and consistently accompanied them through later, more complex processes.

The UCRUS, meanwhile, began to hold regular meetings, first in the Chemical Workers' Union and then in a community center in front of a worker-recovered factory. It developed links with a series of institutions, such as the University of the Republic's large outreach program, and gained entry to the PIT-CNT as a member "with voice but without vote," since they never reached the requirement of three hundred registered and paid members. This was an important symbolic and material step for the union.[4] The union gained legal status and cemented the positions of president, secretary, and treasurer, who were almost always clasificadores. The union also attracted a diverse group of sympathetic *técnicos* (technical advisers) or *asesores* (advisers) ranging from students and professionals to far-left political activists.

The example of the Brazilian equivalent, the *catadores* movement, was important for the Uruguayans. In 2003, a delegation of over thirty Uruguayan clasificadores traveled to Caxias do Sul for the founding conference of the Red Lacre (the Red Latinoamericana de Recicladores, or Latin American Recyclers' Network). It was then, and in the second conference of 2005, that both clasificadores and the activists who traveled with them were able to observe the impressive infrastructure that the catador cooperative movement in Brazil had managed to establish. This consisted of large recycling plants with technologies that would transport, wash, and press materials, as well as the democratic and organizational infrastructure of collective decision making in formal cooperatives. For the clasificadores in Uruguay, this seemed light years away from the individualistic working practices and precarious working conditions of the landfill. The UCRUS took inspiration from its Brazilian counterpart, which presented itself not as a union but as a movement: the Movimiento Nacional do Catadores de Residuos (MNCR). Both UCRUS and the técnicos, some of whom would later join the department that works with clasificadores within the Uruguayan Ministry of Social Development (MIDES), adopted key aspects of the MNCR's program. This included preclassification by citizens and the establishment of recycling plants managed by catadores/clasificadores in a cooperative fashion. Such activity represents the crucial circulation of ideas and experiences throughout the sector at a regional level.

To synthesize its history during the following years, the UCRUS attempted to represent carreros as well as a growing number who started to form cooperatives, following a model promoted by the MIDES and inspired by neighboring countries (Brazil and Argentina). However, a peculiar dynamic arose wherein a majority of clasificadores continued working individually or in family units with horses and carts while those who opted for cooperatives were joined by political militants, principally from anarchist and Trotskyist traditions, some of whom were former industrial workers with experience in trade union organizing. Similar dynamics have been observed in other contexts, such as that of former Bolivian mine workers in the Cocalero movement or in neighborhood organizations in cities such as El Alto (Lazar 2008). In Uruguay the anarchists, many of them Italian immigrant tradesmen, played an important role in the development of trade unionism; the first Uruguayan trade union federation, the Federación Obrera Regional Uruguaya (FORU, 1905–1923), was explicitly anarchist in orientation (Gonzalez Sierra 1989; Errandonea and Costabile 1968). Anarchist activists within the UCRUS continued a national tradition of labor organizing that favored direct action over negotiation, with these political-militants-turned-clasificadores becoming some of the union's most active members. For analytical purposes, then, we can identity three groups that together composed the UCRUS: clasificadores, activists-turned-clasificadores, and asesores.

While prospective cooperativists were courted by the MIDES and other técnicos, and given training sessions and limited infrastructural support, carreros experienced what union officials described as an alternation between repression and permissiveness from the municipal authorities and the police. The activity of clasificadores collecting recyclable public waste in the streets had been legalized when Tabaré Vázquez, currently serving a second term as Uruguay's president, was first elected as mayor of Montevideo in 1990, standing for the center-left party Frente Amplio. Since the beginning of the 2000s, the Intendencia had carried out surveys of clasificadores and begun to regulate their activity, distributing cards and registration plates to clasificadores that allowed them to circulate in the city (while simultaneously prohibiting the activity of those without them). Yet certain arteries of the city were closed to them, such as the principal city-center thoroughfare Avenida 18 de Julio and the coastal road called the *rambla*. Being banned from these streets was not hugely disadvantageous for clasificadores, and it was generally accepted that it was necessary for traffic purposes (the rambla in particular was high-speed and narrow). The denial of access to entire neighborhoods, however—so-called exclusion zones—was different, as was the case with the affluent central neighborhood of Pocitos. As a pilot scheme, the Intendencia set up a system of domestic waste classification with corresponding bins in these areas; the recyclables were picked up by municipal workers and taken to clasificador cooperatives. This was in effect a trial run of what would later come to the Ciudad Vieja.

Alongside restrictions on circulation, it was often the municipal confiscation of horses and carts that most challenged the clasificadores' livelihoods and brought them onto the streets. The confiscation was justified with reference to supposed traffic infringements or mistreatment of horses, but clasificadores claimed that the process was unjust and arbitrary. It was a period of severe repression in 2008, during Ricardo Ehrlich (Frente Amplio)'s reign as mayor, that led to the march that became the other UCRUS event El Abuelo constantly celebrated: "The famous 13th of February, 2008, arrived. Faced with the indiscriminate confiscation [of horses and carts], a demonstration took place which was so important that during the negotiations the repression didn't stop immediately but loosened and loosened—the repressive impetus was extinguished and [the clasificadores] could continue working in the streets, within certain limits. . . . The march of February 13 was a very significant march since it drove home the rights of the clasificadores and [the idea] that they had a legitimate function."

In this brief history, it is possible to highlight several key characteristics that carried into my period of research and have come to characterize the particular configuration of the UCRUS. First, the union still is, as it has been from the beginning, tasked with representing several groups of clasificadores: those in cooperatives, those at the landfill, and those working in family units with horses and carts. Second, the UCRUS remains composed of clasificadores, activists-turned-clasificadores, and asesores, many of whom have experience in other trade unions. Circulation also continues to play a key role in the union's configuration. First, it is the regional circulation of recycling workers between Uruguay, Brazil, and Argentina that provides the inspiration and content for the UCRUS's program. Second, the right to circulate in the city on horse and cart, without harassment or the confiscation of animals or vehicles, is the key demand of the carreros whom the union represents. At the same time, the principal demand of clasificadores at the landfill is for the reliable circulation of valuable waste material. Circulation of persons and valuable waste material is thus a key *demand* of the union—but in the following section I look at how circulation and blockage can function as important *tactics* as well.

Ethnographic Interlude: "The Nation Was Built on Horseback"

When I arrived back in Montevideo at the end of 2013 to conduct doctoral research, clasificadores were on the march again. Or perhaps, on the trot. I met them in front of Uruguay's Palacio Legislativo, where they had mobilized mostly with horse and cart, traveling from different points throughout the city. The march was a family affair, including young children, adolescents, parents, and grandparents. But the mood was angry. They were protesting a decree proposed by a Frente Amplio councilor in the Junta Departamental (Regional Council), which would prohibit carreros from entering the Ciudad Vieja to collect waste. There were already several central areas of the city in which the clasificadores could not circulate with horse and cart, and a recent decree penalized businesses who gave their waste to informal-sector carreros and not to formally registered trucks.

The Ciudad Vieja prohibition was justified with reference to the narrow, historic streets and the longtime complaint that the clasificadores were an eyesore and left rubbish in the streets after rummaging through containers. The Ciudad Vieja generated valuable waste—in particular its scores of office blocks, which disposed of prized white paper. The problem was that the proposed regulation didn't distinguish between clasificadores who had regular pickups from offices and businesses and those who might pass through on foot to search bins in the hope of finding food or paper or something else of value. Thus, many clasificadores found their quite lucrative routes and longtime relations with clients in jeopardy. Unlike other cases where property speculation and neoliberal governance combine to evict the poor from urban living spaces, here clasificadores were threatened with being evicted from labor circuits and dispossessed of valuable surplus material, whose management and sale would then be transferred to formal-sector businesses.

From the Palacio Legislativo the clasificadores marched to the Junta Departamental. They cut through the main arteries of the city, blocking traffic, until they reached the narrow streets of the Ciudad Vieja where the council is situated. The horses and carts bore diverse and colorful political slogans. On the cart of the interim UCRUS president was scrawled a simple quote from Uruguay's founding father, José Artigas: "The cause of the people does not admit the slightest delay." Flags of Uruguay and the tricolor of Artigas (also used by the Frente Amplio) abounded. On a bicycle and cart one man had written: "We're fighting for our jobs." Another sign read: "My struggle for bread and work continues." On one cart, alongside drawings of horses, was written: "The nation was built on horseback."

Most protesters moved on horse and cart, while others trotted along on horseback. The carts ranged from the simple and workmanlike to the elaborate and ceremonial, with the impressive, adorned brass reins that clasificadores use for special occasions. The younger men were dressed in a popular sports style known as *plancha*; most wore Nike baseball caps. Some combined this with the long hair popular in shantytowns. Some were dark-skinned, but it was mostly due to their aesthetic that they stood out as members of the poor and working classes of Montevideo. The march represented the periphery come to visit the center of the city while its suited businessmen looked on, aghast or bemused. Some speeches were made from horseback. One long-haired and bearded activist shouted that clasificadores and their horses had "the same right to circulate in the city as anyone else in their cars."

While some clasificadores stayed looking after the horses, others streamed inside the Junta Departamental building. There was little security or police presence, and the young men in particular seemed hyped up and excited, knocking things over and pushing into offices. Some councilors rushed for cover, and when the leader of the Frente Amplio in the council, Pablo González, came out to speak to the demonstrators, he was quickly surrounded. A clearly frazzled González, shouting to be heard, told demonstrators that the doors of the council were open but only for those who came to "dialogue with order and respect." Two leaders from the UCRUS put forward their demands to González, but other clasificadores complained that they didn't want "the same representatives as always." Another complained that the UCRUS "wanted to send them to recycling plants." One young activist was extremely agitated, encouraging others to "smash it all up!" Another angry young man outside shouted, "I want to work!"

The UCRUS leaders decided that they should march to the Intendencia, the imposing building that houses the executive branch of the municipal council, situated on central Montevideo's main thoroughfare, Avenida 18 de Julio. One protester, Juan, invited me onto a cart with his son. As we trotted down the street he told me about his years of classifying and how he always tried to attend demonstrations by the UCRUS.

The cavalcade came to a stop outside of the Intendencia, where the clasificadores demanded a meeting with Montevideo's mayor. In the end it was decided that the head of social policy and right-hand woman of the mayor would receive a delegation of female clasificadores. The group started to disperse, but not before something of a "dirty protest" occurred: the horses, stopped for a long time outside the Intendencia, inevitably began to relieve themselves under the eyes of the municipal authorities.

Circulation and Blockage as Method and Tactic

The question of circulation and the threat/opportunity of formalization have been an important part of the struggles of other informal-sector workers, street vendors in particular (Lazar 2008; Hansen, Little, and Milgram 2014). Indeed, carreros were not the only group to have their circulation throughout the city impeded by the municipal authorities in Montevideo during 2014. Street-level car window cleaners, another group whose status as workers was in doubt, faced a new threat to their circulation in the city. In a move that surprised some representatives of Frente Amplio, the minister of the interior and the chief of police had moved jointly to prohibit the activity, referencing the obscure Article 543 of the Municipal Code, which establishes when a pedestrian can circulate on the road. Traffic-light jugglers were also included in this enforcement (or repression), with the justification that many used such traffic-light activity as a cover for robbery. During my fieldwork period, the UCRUS tried to make common cause with these and other informal-sector workers (street vendors in particular) who were under pressure to formalize their activity, launching an ultimately unsuccessful attempt to establish an Informal Workers' Federation.

Yet if the question of circulation was key to the struggles of other informal-sector workers, it was principally clasificadores who enacted circulation as a *method* of protest. Blocking the entry of waste to the municipal landfill had been a successful tactic in 2002, but it had rarely been used by the union or landfill clasificadores since then—although it was often threatened. Since the successful march of 2008, however, horse-and-cart cavalcades became the tactic most associated with the UCRUS, which sometimes organized them several times a year. They were moments when territorially divided clasificadores who worked alone or in small family groups could come together in defense of their common interests.

Marches would often depart from several meeting points, coalesce at the Palacio Legislativo, and then make their way along Avenida 18 de Julio to the Intendencia. On an ordinary working day, the clasificador on horse and cart would be alone, awkwardly making their way through a sea of cars that would speed past, often with complaint. Members of the public might harass the clasificador about the condition of their horse or the fact that the animal should be working at all (or even coming into the city). They would run the risk of an inspector or a policeman confiscating the animal and the cart. And were there to be a traffic accident, carreros could rest assured that the blame would be attributed to them, whatever the circumstances, as amplified newspaper headlines made clear every time such an accident occurred. Some members of the public were of course friendly to the clasificadores, and they had their regular clients who would greet them. But as Pablo, a former carrero, told me, "There's always someone who will shit on your day."

On march day, however, clasificadores had safety in numbers among colleagues, family, and friends. The street belonged to them, and their right to circulate on it was uncontested. The cries of clasificadores as they drove their animals down the normally prohibited Avenida 18 de Julio were joyful. Should any motorist attempt to drive through the midst of their march or abuse them, the united clasificadores could easily confront the aggressor. This was a moment where the "imagined community" (Anderson 1983) of clasificadores could be realized and their numbers complemented by the spectacle of horse-drawn transport. The tactic they used to demand the right to circulate was thus itself a rebellious circulation. Marches are of course a common, if not predominant, protest tactic all over the world. Yet whereas a clear space exists between the tactics and the demands in a march for better working conditions, for higher wages, or against cutbacks, in the case of the "march of the carts" the two coalesce. The tactic is the demand: an unimpeded circulation through the city, free from harassment.

During the course of my 2013–2014 fieldwork, the UCRUS decided to complement marches with another form of protest—that of the roadblock—belatedly adopting the method associated with the *piquetero* movement of unemployed workers in post-crisis Argentina (Epstein 2003, 2009; Svampa 2003, 2004). This was another variation on the theme of circulation, in which the workers did not enact their own circulation but rather obstructed that of the general public by blocking the road with horses and carts. The UCRUS had attempted this tactic in winter 2013 and had then decided to carry out three roadblocks on different days in different parts of the city, to build up momentum for their *marcha de carros* on September 2014. They had to discuss and deal with many difficult questions regarding how strictly a blockage to circulation could be enforced. How could an ambulance be let through? Should an especially irate driver be waved on in order to avoid violence? Should the clasificadores only block intermittently, letting the traffic advance in bursts?

The success of this tactic was variable in 2014, with one roadblock attended by few clasificadores and much media; another by many clasificadores but no media; and a third only by myself and another research student! Regardless of outcome, however, the roadblocks had the effect of imposing upon the public the circulation difficulties that carreros experienced on a daily basis.

Sedentarization

The clasificador with horse and cart traveling through the city maps neatly on to the Deleuzian idea of an assemblage. The philosopher used a similar example, that of the knight, to illustrate the concept, wherein the stirrup binds together a "man-animal symbiosis, a new assemblage of war" (Deleuze and Parnet 1987). In the Uruguayan case, the components of the assemblage were bound together in the word *carrito* (little cart), commonly used to refer both to the clasificadores *and* their mode of transport (as in "the carrito problem"). The common complaint from the public and institutions focused on the circulation of the horse and cart in the city, either because it disrupted transport or because the city was supposedly not the natural environment of the horse. Uruguay's vocal humane society, the Protectora de Animales, was a principal adversary of the UCRUS, especially since the union accused the organization of stealing clasificadores' horses, which were then difficult to trace.[5] Yet the assemblage nature of the carritos meant that there was always a slight ambiguity over whether the objection was against the circulation of animals in the city or of the poor. There is no doubt that some saw the circulation of poor people in dirty clothes, riding horses and rummaging in bins, as an eyesore for tourists and an affront to Montevideo's modernity. A plan to convert some carreros into horse-and-cart tourist guides for the Ciudad Vieja had not been well received by the UCRUS. A more ambitious plan, however, was to relocate carreros to municipal recycling plants, with 128 jobs made available in four plants built during 2014.

The moving of carreros to plants, whether cooperative or municipal, is as much one of sedentarization as it is of collectivization. Mobility and autonomy are important values and practices for carreros, as is not having a boss and setting one's own hours. Although difficult economic circumstances might have driven them into the activity, many of the carreros I interviewed preferred the independence of classifying to the security of the cleaning jobs that were usually the alternative, where they would work long hours for low pay. At least on the horse and cart they were their own masters, had control over their working day, and were sure to bring home not only some money but some *requeche* as well.[6]

In Montevideo, one of the advantages of living in irregular housing settlements was the possibility of animal husbandry. So it was all the more galling for clasificadores that some animal rights activists had come to believe that clasificadores would have to hand in their horses on being accepted for a job at a munici-pal recycling plant.[7] Yet while the Intendencia suggested that the recycling plants were for carreros, many of those who entered the recycling plants were coopera-tivists whose cooperatives had been disbanded. Most carreros had resisted enter-ing a cooperative or a municipal plant and being placed under a roof with twenty other vulnerable subjects earning the minimum wage. They preferred the liberty, solitude, and possibility that, despite repression, were offered by the street.

That is not to say that there were not advantages to either working in a re-cycling cooperative or in a formal recycling plant. Instead, it is to say that many carreros defended their activity with reference to much more than their weekly earnings. It was, as some of them told me, a way of life. Indeed, not all those who attended UCRUS demonstrations on horse and cart worked as carreros at that moment in time. They might instead own a horse and cart and come from the same milieu as clasificadores and attend marches to defend their shared way of life. Such a life was also being undermined by the steady relocation of *asenta-miento* dwellers into formal housing, often through housing cooperatives (most recently through former president Pepe Mujica's popular housing scheme "Plan Juntos"). Many of these new dwellings were apartments, and even when they were houses, animal husbandry was often prohibited. Even if clasificadores could keep their horses in *asentamientos*, though, things nevertheless became more dif-ficult if they could not use them as part of their livelihood. As much as they enjoyed using their horses for leisure, carreros were poor and often had many mouths to feed at home. If the horse could be used as a means of transport and a breadwinner, its possession was a lot easier to justify in precarious circumstances.

Some UCRUS militants described the carrero as a modern descendant of the gaucho, the mythical nomadic horseman who roamed Argentina and Uruguay until the land was fenced off and enclosed into private ranches (Ras 1996). The gaucho found a modern descendant in the countryside as well: rural workers, complete with traditional attire and a stronger tradition of horsemanship. During one march, the UCRUS was lent the support of a few horsemen by a rural orga-nization, and they became celebrities of the march. The rural horsemen and the clasificadores of the urban periphery came together every year at El Rusbel, the annual rodeo and horse show that took place at Parque Roosevelt, just outside of Montevideo. In many ways the carreros could trace just as great a cultural and political heritage to the oppressed and marginalized gaucho, who was often treated as a criminal. Like the gaucho, many carreros were also being forced into, and resisting, sedentarization or elimination. It was partly for this reason that in demonstrations the clasificadores clothed themselves in symbols of the nation, to a much greater degree than I witnessed in other political movements. A senior figure at the Intendencia, who was responsible for the municipal management of the recycling plants, argued confidently: "The clasificadores that are in the street today . . . will they be able to continue classifying materials? No, not really. Those who sign up for recycling plants will, but those who don't, will not. Alongside the intermediaries, the profession of informal classification will disappear."

Yet the presence of horses and carts on the streets of Montevideo was surprisingly persistent. Partly this was due to the geographic characteristics of Montevideo, where the distances between center and periphery were not so large as to make them unfeasible for horse and cart. Some thought that the long-held municipal aim of eradicating the carts was a pipe dream and spoke about how, during the dictatorship, police had burned their carts in the street but still had not defeated them. Others were more worried, however, and suggested that while the military had tried a blanket approach, current mayor Ana Olivera was being more "sneaky" by restricting circulation in different areas progressively and rechanneling the circulation of waste so that carreros could not access it. In the following section I turn to look at this circulation of waste.

Mediating Circulation

In another manifestation of the importance of circulation to clasificadores and their union, the UCRUS was often called on to mediate the circulation of surplus waste material between different groups of clasificadores. It can perhaps be argued here that while traditional unions are mostly concerned with the distribution and contestation of surplus value, the UCRUS was concerned with the adjudication and circulation of "surplus material" (Gille 2010). While the UCRUS was at times invited to intervene in disputes between individual clasificadores, their routes were widely respected without need for the union, and the UCRUS was in any case too weak during 2014 to be counted upon as a useful intermediary between individuals. During my fieldwork in 2009–2010, when clasificadores from various collectives and cooperatives regularly attended union meetings, UCRUS headquarters did act as a forum for groups to raise issues concerning the circulation of surplus material. For example, the then-president of the Felipe Cardoso Cooperative (COFECA) raised the issue of another cooperative having stolen a delivery of old mattresses from the port and angrily sought redress, since these could be sold for around US$20 apiece.

During 2013–2014, however, the principal point of circulatory conflict was not between cooperatives, which were rapidly being absorbed into municipal plants. Rather it was the carreros who were losing access to routes and pickups. On the one hand, a municipal decree (Decree 34205) prohibited them from picking up commercial waste, which was some of the most valuable. This prohibition was strongly enforced in central parts of the city where there were coveted pickups, and the carreros were being replaced in this activity by formal businesses, which might be intermediaries who registered a truck or, in a few cases, clasificadores with enough capital to obtain one themselves.

This was a tricky enough issue for the UCRUS, where in some cases it was difficult to differentiate between a clasificador with a truck and a small intermediary, but another issue that emerged during the year was even more delicate. The *ley de envases* (packaging law), whose implementation in Montevideo brought about the construction of the recycling plants, stipulated that they could only receive domestic waste. In other regions of Uruguay, this had meant recyclable waste from new containers placed outside large supermarkets, where the public could dispose of recyclables. Yet in what might be considered an extremely cynical move, the Intendencia of Montevideo also replaced containers in the center of the city and the Ciudad Vieja, using the basic classificatory scheme of "dry" recyclables and "wet" organic waste. These new containers had small, sliding mouths that the Intendencia referred to as "antivandalism" and the UCRUS as "anti-poor." In any case, they made it difficult for street clasificadores to access the materials inside, which were instead taken to the newly constructed recycling plants. In effect, the Intendencia was rechanneling waste materials away from a section of the poor who worked autonomously in the informal sector and toward poor but waged clasificadores working in formal-sector municipal recycling plants.

While attempting to represent clasificadores from both the street and the recycling plants, the UCRUS was not unaware of the dilemmas that these containers posed, and they criticized them for pitting "poor against poor." One irony was that the plant clasificadores did not particularly desire the containers at all, since they brought mixed waste of little value from a public not used to separating their waste into recyclables and nonrecyclables. Yet the plants still received them, and the UCRUS attempted to organize meetings and rallies combining both those who were profiting from the adapted circulation of this waste and those who were being put at a disadvantage. Their position was to oppose the new containers but at the same time lobby the municipal government to improve the value of waste delivered to plants. UCRUS's dilemma was having to represent informal-sector workers alongside those being incorporated into the formal sector and thereby put into competition with their former colleagues. With many national and international trade-union federations intent on campaigning for the transition of informal workers to the formal sector, the problem of dual representation is surely shared by other unions.

Mobile Unionism

Thus far, I have focused on circulation and blockage as key UCRUS tactics whose aim, aside from the performative aspects, is principally to pressure the Intendencia into easing restrictions and allowing unhindered circulation and labor. I have also looked at attempts to sedentarize carreros and how the UCRUS has dealt with the contradictions of the rechanneling of waste circuits. I now turn to the importance of circulation in the everyday organizational work and effectiveness of the union.

During the course of 2014 the UCRUS's weekly meetings at the Galpón de Corrales social center in the working-class district of Villa Española were especially poorly attended, and union officials spoke about holding assemblies in different neighborhoods or rotating meetings to different spaces in order to attract more people. (The city's informal settlements, where most clasificadores lived, were spread out across the city.) The organization of clasificadores by canton was a long-held aim (Fernández 2007, 90), and at times in the past it had been a common practice, as a disaffected UCRUS founder and former president complained: "When I was in the UCRUS, we didn't have meetings there [in Villa Española]. We went around the neighborhoods. Every two weeks we went to a different neighborhood. The place changed. Because . . . the clasificador can't go so far. If you go to the neighborhood . . . you're in their territory. . . . They need to come to the neighborhoods because the majority of the carreros are in our neighborhoods. And they don't come!"

Perhaps twenty or more clasificadores attended a meeting at the Galpón during 2014, but this was almost always a single visit. They failed to return, either discouraged by the meetings or because the effort of regular attendance was simply impossible. I was also present on a few occasions when the UCRUS attempted, with mixed results, to circulate in the neighborhoods. They attempted to hold a series of neighborhood assemblies, starting in Marconi. The nature of this first assembly was indicative of the crisis into which the UCRUS had slumped, since Marconi should have been a successful place to meet. Not only was it a neighborhood with a large number of clasificadores, where Padre Cacho had worked and where the UCRUS had held its foundational meeting, it was also where the interim UCRUS president lived. Yet aside from a couple of neighborhood characters who seemed to spend most evenings in the plaza anyway, only a few clasificadores appeared, and union officials were even heckled. The poor quality of the sound equipment meant that it was difficult to make any sense of the interim president's rambling speech.

On another occasion, we headed out to distribute leaflets for the September march in some informal settlements in the east of Montevideo. Clasificadores' homes were usually fairly obvious, as materials were stacked up in their yards and they had horses in ramshackle stables. We also asked around the neighborhood for people who classified, whereupon we would usually be pointed in the direction of someone or other. This got a better response than the ill-fated assembly in Marconi. It was an occasion when the union officials were able to listen to the stories of the clasificadores. Had they been affected by prohibition from parts of the city? What did they think of the new recycling plants? How was the market in materials looking? It was also a chance for the union to report back on its activity, encourage clasificadores to attend union meetings, and gauge their opinion on possible actions. Clasificadores were friendly, committing themselves to organizing their neighborhoods and attending the next march. Some offered tips: Nobody seemed to be taking much notice of the marches these days; what about another tactic? The president spoke of the roadblocks and of combining a march with a camp or hunger strike, while another clasificador recommended obstructing the entrance of waste materials to Felipe Cardoso. Such encounters demonstrated the potential of the union reaching out to the neighborhoods and circulating in them, but they were the exception. In general, the UCRUS continued with poorly attended weekly meetings.

When I worked at the recycling cooperative COFECA and they were coordinating with the UCRUS on the eve of their move to the Geminis recycling plant, the morning appearances of El Abuelo were ironically a sign both of his own vitality and the frailty of the union. The eighty-five-year-old would take a bus or two and then walk from Camino Carrasco the length of Felipe Cardoso to arrive at COFECA. Several times he appeared alone, and the others complained that it was always El Abuelo who came by himself: where was the rest of the union? At another meeting, a clasificador ally turned up with another of his neighbors. He was meant to be meeting the secretariat to talk about organizing, but only El Abuelo and I were present. This longtime supporter challenged El Abuelo as to why there were not more people present after twelve years of the union's existence, and the union stalwart struggled to answer the question.

Of course, it is not fair to accuse the other union leaders of being immobile, and the extremely leaky and noisy but colorful shell of the Galpón de Corrales hardly represented the pinnacle of union opulence or aristocracy. Instead, the union had threadbare militants during 2014 who attempted to spread themselves thin. No member of the secretariat possessed a car, or even a motorbike, so most made their way around walking, cycling, or on public transport. They were only paid a small amount for union work, which they had to combine with a range of other activities (unlike El Abuelo, who was retired). The interim president's time became even more restricted when he accepted a well-paid temporary job as a security guard on a building site in his neighborhood. The longtime and respected secretary attempted to combine her union work with a job as a caregiver and ended up having to resign from the latter because of her commitment to union activity. She suffered from back problems, in large extent due to a life of hard work classifying on the streets. They all relied, where possible, on transport with the PIT-CNT representative, the only one of the regular UCRUS attendees who had a car. The circulation of union officials, regarded as key for successfully mobilizing their sector, was thus restrained by their own precarious economic situations and ill health.

Sedentary Unionism

It is perhaps useful at this point to reflect on how different this situation is from that of a traditional, workplace trade union. Militancy and trade union involvement of course depends hugely on the sector and epoch (Gall 2002). Trade unions are in most cases forced to engage in recruitment (Mason and Bain 1991; Kelly and Heery 1989), but in a regular scenario, a trade union member would approach the union with a complaint or issue. In the case of UCRUS, not only does it not have a fixed list of members who pay a subscription (the union is in principal tasked with representing *every* clasificador), it must also go to the clasificador in their neighborhood. It is resented if it does not—and even sometimes when it does. While other trade unions have offices and headquarters, UCRUS unionists are expected to ambulate throughout the city, conducting a mobile unionism.

Returning to the key demand of the UCRUS, that of the right to circulate freely throughout the city collecting materials, it is clear that this is also hugely different from the world of pay claims, disputes, strikes, and tribunals of the formal trade union. In this section I would like to compare the mobile unionism of the UCRUS with the sedentary unionism of the trade union federation of which they formed a part, the PIT-CNT. In referring to the PIT-CNT unionists as sedentary, I do not wish to denigrate them but merely to pick up on one of the key definitions of sedentary: "tending to spend much time seated."[8] This characteristic is defining not only of some trade union officials, who inevitably spend much time in meetings, but of millions of other jobs as well and should not carry any connotation of inaction. Rather, I wish to contrast the expectations placed on UCRUS militants with those from the formal trade-union sector, in which the UCRUS operated rather uncomfortably.

The year of 2014 was particularly sedentary for the PIT-CNT. It was an election year, and the links between the union federation and the governing Frente Amplio were becoming increasingly corporatist (see Silverman 2011). While UCRUS activists spoke of how the clasificadores had to put pressure on politicians to gain commitments during this period, sources within the PIT-CNT told them that they wouldn't be organizing any demonstrations or marches that might challenge the government or upset the chances for a Frente Amplio victory, as a lackluster presidential campaign from former president Tabaré Vázquez faced a challenge from Luis Alberto Lacalle Pou, the youthful if vacuous son of former neoliberal president Luis Alberto Lacalle. Successive Frente Amplio governments had brought about improvements in workers' rights and conditions, with particular victories being the institution of the eight-hour rural working day and the recent introduction of legislation that enabled neglectful businesses to be criminally charged for the death or injury of a worker. In addition, nine members of the secretariat of the PIT-CNT featured as candidates for the Frente Amplio in their national lists in 2014. The only action the union took during the election period was an electoral stoppage to declare support for a Frente Amplio government and opposition to a government of the two center-right parties, all the while declaring its "class independence."

When the UCRUS did go to the PIT-CNT's headquarters, as they did for a period during my fieldwork, it was either to attend meetings of the health, safety, and environment committee (under whose banner they fell) or to be heard at the federation's executive committee. The attempts to attend the executive proved rather confusing and exacerbated some of the insecurities of the UCRUS and its relation to the federation. The UCRUS asked the committee to put out a statement supporting them on three key points. The first was that it publicly oppose plans for the incineration of waste; the second that it oppose the decree that barred carreros from collecting commercial waste; and the third that it support a plan for a levy on plastic bags, which would pay dignified salaries to clasificadores in a larger recycling plant.

UCRUS activists had received a text telling them to attend the PIT-CNT executive meeting, which would give them a response, and had duly turned up only to be kept waiting for several hours. Executive committee members occasionally came and went from the meeting upstairs, but no one in the UCRUS knew who had sent the text message, and neither did the executive committee seem to know anything about it. UCRUS militants complained about how they were being treated, until eventually we were ushered up to the large meeting room, where twenty delegates from different trade unions were gathered around a table. The secretary apologized for the confusion, explaining that they were awaiting a report from the health, safety, and environment committee before making any decisions. We were asked to return the following week, when again we had to wait several hours before we were allowed to go up to the meeting room, where UCRUS officials were asked to introduce the issues relevant to their sector. In the end, the PIT-CNT's response was to arrange meetings with both the presidency and the Intendencia to discuss these issues, while quietly voicing support.

The way in which the UCRUS perceived their reception by the PIT-CNT and the confused manner in which the UCRUS presented their case signified not only the precariousness of the UCRUS leadership but also that of their link with the PIT-CNT, despite how proud they were of that link (by which they had been recognized, as the UCRUS secretary told me, as "workers like any other"). During the course of my fieldwork, UCRUS militants were uncomfortable with sedentary union practices, such as negotiations with the Intendencia, that were secured after the September march. During four sets of tripartite meetings between the Intendencia, UCRUS, and PIT-CNT, the union failed to make any headway on the seven-point program they took into the meetings, and there was soon talk of more demonstrations, marches, and hunger strikes.

The comparison between the UCRUS and the PIT-CNT can be set in the context of the history of Uruguayan trade unionism. In the early twentieth century, militant anarchist trade unions predominated (most within the FORU), in what Errandonea and Costabile (1968) classify as an "oppositional model" of trade unionism, where militant strike action was often the first option. In contrast, these authors chart the slow emergence of "dualist" trade unions, which might have a revolutionary or radical leadership but engage with more immediate concerns of the workers. For these, strike action was a last resort (see the dual role of unions in Darlington 2014, 113). Although there are clear differences in the sector represented (the FORU mostly represented skilled artisans with significant leverage), there are also clear continuities with the anarchist-influenced UCRUS's preference for direct action over negotiation.[9]

Conclusion

The focus on circulation in this chapter emerged from the simple demand of car-reros to be able to circulate in the city, including in the most affluent and waste-rich areas, without harassment. However, it soon became clear that circulation was important for the UCRUS in many other ways as well, from the regional circulation of recycler activists that inspired its program to the tactic of blockage and circulation through which it acted out its demands or otherwise pressured the municipal government. The UCRUS had to deal with the municipal rechanneling of waste from poor workers in the informal sector to those recently incorporated into the formal sector while simultaneously attempting to represent all clasificadores, from plant workers and cooperativists to those working at the landfill, on horse and cart, on bicycle, or on foot.

Negotiating the circulation and distribution of surplus *material*, instead of disputing the allocation of surplus *value*, is perhaps peculiar to the recycling sector, in Uruguay and beyond. Yet in struggling over the right to circulate in the city—to work as well as live in areas like Montevideo's Ciudad Vieja that are targeted for speculation, development, tourism, or gentrification—clasificadores make common cause with the urban poor worldwide. In place of the negotiation tactics of sedentary unionism, the UCRUS has drawn on the Uruguayan anarchist tradition to advocate direct action and on national history and myth to create a comparison between their struggle and that of the dispossessed but autonomous gauchos of lore.

Like other post-dictatorship Latin American countries under center-left governments, the UCRUS had to tackle forms of repression that were insidious but not flagrantly brutal. Clasificador carts were no longer burned in the street (although they might still be confiscated), but businesses were now penalized for giving their waste to informal-sector waste workers. Rather than having to defend their ward against wholesale criminalization, the UCRUS had to navigate a complex, evolving sector where some clasificadores were given "dignified," if low-paid, jobs in recycling plants, while the unlucky ones were simply dispossessed of their livelihoods. (And this while operating in conditions of precarious health and economic circumstance.)

During the course of the year, it became clear that the union was struggling, despite the best efforts of the small team of activists who sustained it and tried to organize the sector during a difficult year. While clasificadores and the UCRUS performed their right to circulate in periodic marches, and there were no reports of carreros surrendering their horses on going to work in plants, union informants felt that longtime efforts to sedentarize the nomadic carreros were finally making some headway. The presence of the poor circulating in the center of the city was being diminished, as has been the case in other Latin American capitals (Medina 2000, 52). As the UCRUS secretary told me, if she wasn't able to access valuable waste in affluent Pocitos, what would she go there for? *To go for a walk?*

From feelings of autonomy, work in family units, and relations of patronage with informal-sector intermediaries, those who found a place in a municipal plant would now have to deal with the implications of formal work, a steady minimum wage, and being considered vulnerable social subjects with "protected jobs." And the union would have to adapt accordingly.[10]

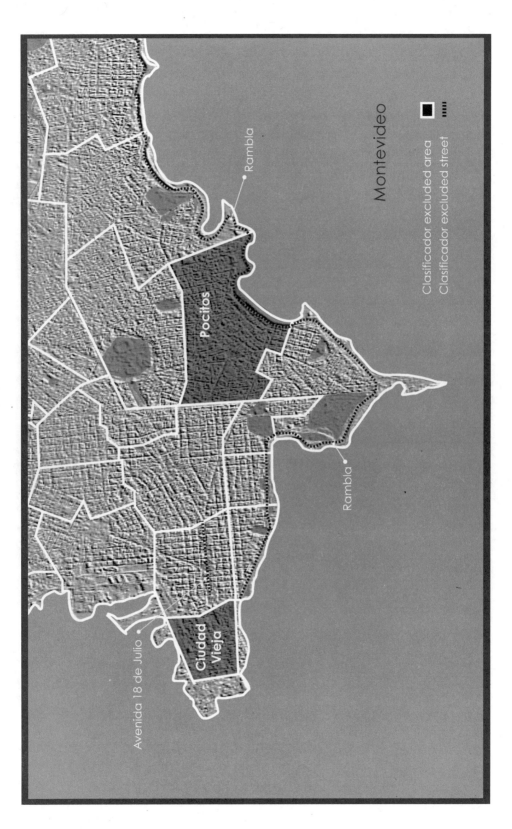

Rambla

Pocitos

Rambla

Avenida 18 de Julio

Ciudad Vieja

Montevideo

Clasificador excluded area
Clasificador excluded street

Above: The green flag of the UCRUS (*bottom, center left*) flies among other flags and banners at the PIT-CNT's 2014 May Day celebration. *Facing page, top*: Young clasificadores on the march from the Palacio Legislativo. The UCRUS secretary argued that prohibiting their activity would push young clasificadores into crime. *Facing page, bottom*: Clasificadores wait outside the Junta Departamental while a charged confrontation with local councilors takes place inside. (All photos for this chapter by Patrick O'Hare; map by M. D. Freedman.)

Part III:
Urban Squatter Movements in South Asia:
Kolkata and Jakarta

Chapter 7

The Nonadanga Eviction in Kolkata

Contemporary Urban Development and People's Resistance[1]

Swapna Banerjee-Guha

On March 30, 2012, a state-initiated slum demolition drive took place at Nonadanga, located in the southeastern part of Kolkata near the Eastern Metropolitan Bypass. More than eight hundred slum houses were bulldozed by the police, with indiscriminate torching of huts in and around the area. A procession organized in protest on April 4 by slum dwellers, sympathizers, and democratic-rights organizations was brutally attacked by the police, leaving a large number injured. In protest, a sit-in was organized on April 8 at Nonadanga that was attended by a larger number. The police did not spare them either. Nearly seventy protestors were arrested. Among them seven members of various left and democratic-rights organizations were slapped with false charges and denied bail for several months. The following day, April 9, about 115 people were arrested at a protest meeting on College Street—the hub of Kolkata's youth revolts.

The Nonadanga eviction and associated police atrocities once again brought to light the willingness of the state machinery in West Bengal to pursue a development path that not only does not recognize the right of the poor to the city but shows a thorough disregard for their right to rehabilitation in the event of development-induced displacements. The brutality of the eviction is the state's way of

137

affirming that the poor are absolutely nonessential in the current city development framework, no matter what the rehabilitation policy says. The country's National Relief and Rehabilitation Policy of 2007 states that before any development projects are finalized the state needs to minimize displacement, promote nondisplacing or least-displacing alternatives (as far as possible), or offer adequate rehabilitation measures, especially to the weaker classes. This must be done prior to displacement, if displacement is unavoidable. The detention of the protesters of the Nonadanga eviction and their subsequent harassment indicate the manner in which the state government is going to deal with resistance to such development schemes. It is interesting to see how systemic the tyrannical stance of the state is in such cases.

Whether such development projects are being pursued by the present government of West Bengal, which justifies its intentions by appealing to *maa* (mother), *maati* (land), and *manush* (people), or by a group like the previous one, which used to invoke a specific political philosophy to articulate its concern for the poor, by now it is clear that the beneficiaries of these projects are not the masses of the common people or the poor. The purpose of these projects is to make the cities more attractive for the rich and induce more and more corporate groups to invest. The motive is to persuade them to buy more property, invest in land and real estate, and invest in the IT or IT-enabled services sectors that will further consolidate the power of affluent classes in the cities. Does this make the cities better and more livable for the large majority? No. Ready examples are Mumbai, Delhi, and several other cities where since the late 1990s several hundred thousand slum-dwelling families have been displaced in order to make way for development projects.

Actually, the victims of such development ventures are inevitably the poor and the underprivileged, who are always the first to be uprooted and dispossessed. They are forced to surrender their right to the city where they have been living or working for years, yielding the space to projects that will make the city more beautiful and expensive, so that one day they will have no other option but to move even farther away—out to distant peripheries with fewer and fewer prospects of survival. Sometimes their right to the city is taken away by the logic of the market, abetted by the state; sometimes by direct government action that expels them from their homes; and sometimes by illegal means like violence or arson. In Mumbai, slum fires in areas like Bandra and Andheri (where the land value is very high) are a recurrent affair. The Nonadanga atrocity and subsequent state repression have only served to reiterate the viewpoint of the state machinery in India with respect to the prevailing development path and its associated projects. Individuals, groups, and democratic-rights organizations questioning the justifiability of such projects, whether in the cities, in the villages, or in the forests, are branded as antinationals or terrorists.

Making Kolkata a "World-Class City"

Since its formation in 2011, the new West Bengal government began announcing its urban vision of converting Kolkata into a world-class city, with London as its model (for reasons known best to the government and its urban experts). Accordingly, it has been formulating a series of plans for beautification and upscaling through numerous projects. Several parts of the city are getting earmarked for smartening; a number of buildings are being given a facelift; the Ganga riverfront is being developed as an expanded space of leisure (modeled on that of the Thames in London); a number of entry gates are being planned in different locations in the city; unused tram compartments are getting converted into cafeterias or banquet halls, the latter obviously for corporate use; and vigorous drives have been launched to give a free hand to real estate for constructing gigantic commercial and residential complexes in discrete locations, often displacing the poor who have been living and working in these areas for decades. Kolkata now boasts of having the largest mall in eastern India.

Are these projects a novel idea of the current government of West Bengal? Are they unique to Kolkata? In both cases the answer is no. The previous West Bengal government, led by a coalition of the organized Left, had enthusiastically introduced similar urban development programs that were also associated with displacement and eviction, following the prescription of the Jawaharlal Nehru Urban Renewal Mission (JNNURM): the first and the largest postindependence urban planning initiative in the country. And again, Kolkata is not the only city where such beautification drives are seen. One city after another, in different parts of the country, has joined the bandwagon, under the diktat of the JNNURM, Mumbai, and Delhi leading the march. Restructuring in Kolkata is only a part of a larger program framed by the doctrines of a neoliberal ideology, the imperatives stemming from the nexus of big capital, international financial institutions, and the state machinery.

Neoliberal Urbanism in India

To understand, we have to go back to the 1980s. With the introduction of the new economic policy in 1991, Indian cities—like many other cities of the developing world—entered into a global framework and started getting reshaped according to the exigencies of global capital. But the beginning of the story goes further back, to when the groundwork was being planned. Externally assisted urban-sector projects in India have accounted for more than US$230 million since independence. In the Seventh National Plan (1985–90), for the first time a special emphasis was put on private investment in urban development. In support, the National Commission on Urbanisation in 1985 ushered in a major shift in the country's urban policy—from decentralization to centralization—and advocated for private-sector entry into urban service provision. Accordingly, in 1991, the Mega City Programme of the central government was launched to revamp the infrastructure of large cities with more private-sector investment. The commission's report was followed by the 74th Constitutional Amendment Act in 1992 (Banerjee-Guha 2009a), which drastically reduced state funding for municipalities and forced them to turn to capital in order to raise funds for development projects, obviously compromising on the pro-poor agenda. Subsequently, in 1996, the Expert Group on Commercialisation of Infrastructure estimated the required investment in urban infrastructure at around Rs 250,000 crore for the coming ten years.[2] This made the entry of private capital into urban development an even more pressing necessity, as it had already been announced that the government lacked funds. A major overhauling of the administrative and legislative frameworks was suggested to smooth the way for involving international financial institutions like the World Bank, the Asian Development Bank, the United States Agency for International Development, and the United Kingdom's Department for International Development in the drafting of India's urban reforms mandate. Finally, in 2005, the JNNURM took official shape, its name invoking Jawaharlal Nehru, the first prime minister of independent India from the original Congress Party.

Detailed plans were chalked out to equip the cities to function as nodes of global finance acceptable to the credit-rating agencies. A mandatory decoration of the cityscape was prescribed, in the interest of making it more beautiful and therefore investment-friendly. It was initially in large cities that privatization of the service delivery system was introduced, but this subsequently expanded to medium and small cities, depending on their location. At the same time the concept of "private cities" was brought in, in total opposition to the concept of planned towns that was earlier developed by state planning organizations across the country as a way to provide housing to those in middle- and lower-income groups. The new private cities started being developed entirely by real-estate firms with only basic infrastructural support from the state. An aggressive—almost revanchist—urban development program was introduced all over the country in the form of gigantic infrastructure and real-estate projects targeting a small section of the elite as the chosen clientele. For all these projects, whether restructuring the existing cities or making new ones, vast tracts of land had to be handed over to the private developers, which made the poor in cities and the small- and medium-scale farmers in the peripheries extremely vulnerable. State-sponsored dispossession became a characteristic feature, with state governments turning into coercive land brokers for capital. People's struggles to protect their right to land in cities thus got linked with a larger struggle coming out from the countryside: to protect agricultural land, a struggle that had already intensified due to the decision of the central and several state governments to build special economic zones (SEZs) across the country (Banerjee-Guha 2008). Land became a key component, in both city and countryside, of an interstate competition to attract private-sector investment that became fiercer day by day. The think tanks like McKinsey Global Institute that loomed behind the city-restructuring initiatives pointed to the urban poor as the biggest impediment to the materialization of megadevelopment projects and recommended drastically reducing the slum-dwelling population from 60% to 10% of the city's inhabitants, which means displacement was not a byproduct but a fundamental component of such initiatives. Following the principles of neoliberalism, the state emerged as a key abettor to all these endeavors and framed new legalities to aid the process vociferously. Developmental governance became a catchword. Pitched heavily on the rationality of experts and professionals (Sanyal 2007), it made use of extra-coercive mechanisms, incorporating a wide range of institutional and social forces based on an alliance of state, capital, and civil society to facilitate a neoliberal development path. The tentacles of this alliance operated well beyond government mechanisms and earned multiscalar relational governance the faith of a large section of the affluent middle class in addition to the rich. As part of the new governance, several NGOs were co-opted (like Janaagraha in Bangalore) and even started conducting workshops to convince people of the efficacy of private-public partnership projects (Benjamin 2010). The backtracking of the state from active engagement in providing housing and basic infrastructures became an accepted reality. It is interesting to see how the Indian state mobilized all these forces to justify the scheme of modernizing cities and making them pivotal spaces for capital accumulation. Careful analysis shows that the timing of the introduction of JNNURM coincided with a number of other anti-people blueprints under the new economic policy.

It is therefore necessary to understand that this new urban order is intertwined with a larger restructuring of the economy characterized by increased commodification, shrinking of the organized sector, hyperexploitation of workers, downgrading of democratic rights earned through long struggles, and last but not least a tremendous economic uncertainty (Banerjee-Guha 2009b). The aggressive vision of redesigning Indian cities in the above manner rests in its central elements on the shift of capital from the primary circuit of production to the secondary circuit of built environment (Harvey 1985). The consequences can be seen in the increasing focus on hyperforms and megaconstruction activities trending toward sterility and sameness (Chatterton 2002); increased speculation and expanded investment in land, real estate, and the service sector; and signature projects, coupled with a reduced focus on employment-generating production processes, affordable housing, and collective sharing of urban space and resources.

Revanchist Urban Renewal Mission: Operational Framework

Let us look at the operational framework of the JNNURM in order to contextualize the increasing vulnerability of the poor in Nonadanga and the other slums of Kolkata (and in the slums of several other cities as well). The Mission was classified into two parts. Sub-mission A, entitled Urban Infrastructure and Governance, accounted for 65% of the initial total funds of Rs 50,000 crore and was administered by the Ministry of Urban Development. All infrastructure and beautification projects came under this heading. Let me mention here that in the Eleventh National Plan, public-private partnership was accepted as the prime option to fund infrastructure projects, following which the infrastructure budget rose sharply from Rs 260 crore in 2007–08 to a whopping Rs 560 crore in 2011–12. A crucial fact in this respect is that with the introduction of JNNURM, real estate was given an incredible boost by allowing 100% foreign direct investment (FDI).

Sub-mission B, entitled Basic Services to the Urban Poor (BSUP), accounted for the remaining 35% of the funds and was administered by the Ministry of Urban Employment and Poverty Alleviation. Slum improvement and rehabilitation as well as access to basic services fell under its purview. All previous central government schemes for the urban poor thus got annulled and brought under the Mission. The involvement of two separate ministries with divergent foci, however, exposed a deep anomaly in the structure and purpose of the Mission. Proposals given priority were all from Sub-mission A, incorporating mega-infrastructure projects, gigantic commercial and residential complexes, shopping malls, cultural "signature" projects, and urban spectacles. Funds were regularly released for these projects, while Sub-mission B projects struggled to gain acceptance and funding allotment. Also, while the infrastructure budget steadily increased (Government of India 2008), BSUP funds never experienced any rise. A drastic shift from provision of basic services and low-cost housing to market-driven projects was under way, the latter taking the lion's share of the JNNURM budget. Where was the space for the poor in this grandiose scheme? One must note that one of the official agendas of the Mission was to make cities "slum-free" over a period of time. The Mission efficiently worked toward intensifying social inequality through an imposing planning mechanism, helping cities gradually get rid of the poor from vital locations and thereby raise property values in all such areas.

The stated aim of the Mission was to bestow "world-class" status on—initially—sixty-three cities by building infrastructure: wide roads, overpasses, tunnels, skywalks, large-scale commercial blocks, and gigantic residential, recreational, and entertainment complexes. The vision was the same for all cities, large and small, and all reforms were mandatory. To access funds, the state governments had to set up para-statal bodies that would evaluate project proposals and release (and even manage) funds. Infrastructure, commercial, and cultural projects funded and implemented by the private sector were given priority. In conjunction with this scheme, the central government's National Common Minimum Programme made necessary arrangements to bring land and housing within the orbit of the market and paved the way for 100% FDI in urban infrastructure. To access Mission funds, municipalities were required to prepare a city development plan: a twenty-five-year vision document defining the direction they wanted to pursue. Most plans were ready within a month and got evaluated by hired private bodies. Within three months, Rs 86,482.95 crores for twenty-three projects was released. All former schemes, like the National Slum Development Programme, Swarna Jayanti Shahari Rozgar Yojana, Valmiki Ambedkar Awas Yojana (for housing the socially marginalized and urban poor), national transportation policy, and so forth were brought under the Mission.

A careful look at JNNURM shows that essentially it was a reform-linked urban investment program of private capital. Based on subtle forms of competition, place-marketing, and regulatory undercutting for attracting investment, it involved a range of conditionalities, the key items being privatization and commercialization of basic services; liberalization of land and real estate through repeal of the Urban Land Ceiling and Regulation Act (ULCR); changes in rent control legislation; development of a strong mortgage market with 100% FDI in housing and real estate; easier land use conversion norms; reforms in property tax; financial and administrative restructuring of municipalities; outsourcing of municipal services by cutting down organized jobs; introduction of e-governance; and valorization of the private sector and private credit-rating agencies over elected civic bodies (CASUMM 2006). The sweeping transformation of governance was meant to cripple municipal bodies and encroach upon the constitutionally devolved areas of state government jurisdictions, modalities often governed by the corporate sector. Take the case of repealing ULCR. The act was passed in 1976 to prevent the concentration of land in the hands of speculative capital. A ceiling was subsequently introduced on the ownership of vacant urban land to make more such lands available for the poor. In 1999, the central government abolished the act. Until 2005 it was still a vital piece of legislation at the state level for making surplus land available at affordable prices. JNNURM made the repeal of the act mandatory for accessing Mission funds and in the process brought huge quantities of land into the market that had earlier accommodated poor people's housing. Since late 1990s more than 200,000 families have been evicted from such lands in Delhi; in Mumbai, in 2005 alone, more than 90,000 slum units were demolished (CASUMM 2006). National Building Organization data showed that among the 24.7 million people rendered homeless in 2006, more than 97% were the urban poor (Singh 2008). The reconstruction of urban space through displacement and dispossession had already been facilitated by measures of the new economic policy, creating tremendous economic uncertainty among the working class and the poor. Closures of factories and mills, restrictions on small-scale manufacturing and retail units, regulations against informal workers, and privatization of basic services like water, sanitation, housing, and health were a few such measures. With the apparent aim of regenerating declining industrial areas and creating jobs in the "dynamic" sectors of culture and leisure, in city after city the new projects started enclosing spaces long used by the people, particularly the poor. To preclude resistance, new zoning laws were enacted; surveillance stepped up, targeting hawkers, rag pickers, and vendors who were labeled encroachers on public land (Banerjee-Guha 2010).

Judging by its impact in several cities, a persistent fact that gets reiterated about the Mission is its systematic contribution to aggravating inequality: making the disadvantaged classes more vulnerable. That this constitutes the fundamental core of neoliberalism (Harvey 2005) and not its byproduct needs thorough exposure. When government's very purpose is to facilitate neoliberal capitalist accumulation, it is obvious that the poor, who have been facing dispossession due to socioeconomic restructuring in various forms, will slide further down in the remade urban landscapes (Smith 2002). Interventions through laws and regulations by the state and collateral organizations have only strengthened this exclusionist mechanism. The exact mix of market, monopolistic control, and state intervention, however, has varied from city to city in service to the social reproduction patterns of each region, going on to make a series of subsystems separated from each other by regional competitive barriers but concurrently connected through a wider neoliberal ideology.

After a change in central government in 2014, JNNURM was initially extended until 2015. In April 2015 Prime Minister Modi renamed JNNURM as the Atal Mission for Rejuvenation and Urban Transformation (AMRUT), after Atal Bihari Vajpayee, a former prime minister from the Bharatiya Janata Party. For AMRUT, the allotted budget is Rs 50,000 crore to be spent over a period of five years on five hundred select cities. Until 2017, these funds will go to support JNNURM projects that are already 50% complete, along with projects in a few other cities judged to have touristic prospects and commercially and industrially advantageous locations. The previous government had done all the preparatory work for a JNNURM phase two, selecting five hundred cities for transformation and adding the new concept of the "Smart City"—selecting a few new private cities and some existing ones for smartening. AMRUT has become the new avatar of JNNURM, keeping its focus and the purpose the same. The cabinet meeting that cleared AMRUT sanctioned Modi's dream project of Smart Cities too. With a budget of Rs 48,000 crore, Smart Cities will smarten a hundred select cities across the country to optimize efficiency in urban services by using technology. Having a "local-area-based approach," it will also support the local distinctiveness of the existing settlements. The routine rhetoric is identical to that of JNNURM phase two. In reality the concept is intended to make cities more economically competitive, especially in relation to cities of the developed world (Burte 2014). Operational and economic efficiency are the factors that will enhance the capacity of the cities to attract business, making information and communication technologies the central aspect of smartness (Hollands 2008). But in this smart vision, where is the space for ordinary citizens and the poor, who have less technology access but whose contribution to the cities' economic life is nevertheless undeniable?

The making of nearly four hundred SEZs across the country has already become a critical phenomenon in the development scenario of India. With the implementation of JNNURM followed by AMRUT and the Smart City Mission, land acquisition has taken a new turn, making people's right to land more critical than ever before. Acquisition of peasant lands for the corporate sector to make SEZs and private cities in recent times has been identified as a new phase of primitive accumulation (Patnaik 2008) wherein lands are used more for corporate real estate and speculation than for economic activities that can generate more employment.

The colonial Land Acquisition Act of 1894 was the primary law of land acquisition in India until 2011 and gave power of eminent domain to the state to acquire any land for "public good." The euphoria with which the Indian state constructed SEZs (the first in 2005) and private cities at the beginning of this century derived institutional support from the colonial act and displaced millions from their land and livelihood, leading to large-scale protests all over the country.

Electoral compulsions finally forced the government to amend the act, and a new Land Acquisition Act was passed in 2013. Despite making considerable allowance for land acquisition for "public purpose" (to be solely defined by the government) and violating several safeguarding clauses for the poor (Banerjee-Guha forthcoming), the new act failed to satisfy the corporate groups that continued to press for further dilution of the clauses requiring consent (from the users of the land) and rehousing (of the affected families). A major step toward appeasing the corporate sector that the new government took after assuming office in 2014 was to pass an ordinance diluting the above clauses in the line of corporate demand. This ordinance has yet to be cleared by the parliament.

Excluding the Poor: Nonadanga and Beyond

Against this backdrop, we go back to the Nonadanga residents. Nonadanga is an area chosen in 2007 as one of the BSUP resettlement sites for slum dwellers who had been evicted from different parts of the city to make way for implementing the Sub-mission A projects of the JNNURM and other, similar infrastructure schemes that were then being implemented in Kolkata and other areas. Many came in 2009 from the Sundarbans when the devastating hurricane Aila struck the entire deltaic region of South Bengal. Many others came from Singur and Nandigram when the previous state government decided to hand over their agricultural land to the Tatas and other corporate groups for industrial development. The resettlement project in Nonadanga has been officially and jointly run by the Kolkata Metropolitan Development Authority (KMDA) and the Kolkata Environmental Improvement Project, the latter being the owner of the land. The residents have been eking out a living by working informally in various organizations or as domestic workers, rickshaw pullers, construction workers, car drivers, vegetable sellers, security guards, and so on. While they live in abject poverty, their contribution to the city's economy is unquestionable. No funds from Sub-mission B (BSUP) have been allocated to provide basic infrastructure, schools, or health facilities in the resettlement area. (Whether the funds were not released or were released but remained unutilized is a different question altogether, into which we cannot enter now.) Initially, in 2007, the KMDA built a few small, one-room apartments, but did not continue with the scheme.

As the settlement grew, many more displaced families from different parts of the city or from outside have come in, settled down in vacant spaces, made their own shanties, and developed a system of community living. They gave names to the different segments of their settlement, like "Shramik" (Worker) Colony or "Mazdur

Palli" (Laborer Village), articulating their identity as workers (P. S. Roy, unpublished notes). Nonadanga residents have gone through cycles of displacements: first, when they came to Kolkata having been uprooted from their original homes; then again when their slum lands were taken away for development projects—often several times over. They have resettled multiple times and rebuilt their lives each time they got uprooted, only to lose them again. The final blow came in 2012. I have mentioned that the KMDA had stopped building apartments a long while back in Nonadanga. In 2012, it decided to enter into a public-private partnership housing project allowing the developer to use a large part of the land for commercial ventures. Before handing over the land to the private developer, KMDA wanted the area to be free of "encroachers," which led to the eviction drive.

From late 2011 onward the entire area of Nonadanga started experiencing a commercial boom. With the real estate goons having their eye on Nonadanga and the surrounding neighborhood, all of a sudden the residents who had been officially allotted land under the BSUP provisions of the JNNURM were turned into illegal encroachers who, according to the state machinery, could only deserve expulsion, and that without any official notice. Goons of the ruling political party who had once allowed these people to build their hutments in lieu of "protection money" now joined the government to oust them. The urban development minister ordered expulsion of all illegal encroachers by March 30, 2012. The consequent eviction drive that I have discussed was especially ruthless as the residents demanded proper rehabilitation. The police and ununiformed goons brutally attacked the residents; women and children were not spared. KMDA men and the goons looted all their belongings, including their house-building materials (tarpaulin and bamboo) and even their voter identity cards and ration cards, to destroy the proof of their legal status. Naturally, no seizure list was made. The supporting protesters, too, were treated in an extremely high-handed manner. The arrested activists who were denied bail and taken into custody were slapped with false charges including sedition and links with "Maoists" (a standard statist practice in West Bengal since the 1970s, from the time of the Naxalbari uprising, and subsequently in several other states, used to suppress antistate protests by intellectuals, students, professionals, and the people at large).

The Nonadanga incident exposed the true intent of the present West Bengal government and, for that matter, of any regional government in India with respect to the urban poor. It could not have been otherwise, because any government practicing the formulae of JNNURM and AMRUT with dexterity can have no other approach. The very purpose of these Missions is the promotion of exclusionary urban development, to make cities more habitable for the rich. And this brings us to the issue of the basic right of the people to their cities. Who will decide this right? Who will define it, grant it, or deny it? Who will exercise it?

The resistance that the Nonadanga residents put up in 2009 has no doubt weakened due to internal dissensions, subsequent police repression and intimidation, and physical attacks by ruling party goons. But they have not surrendered or given up their struggle, and they still hold a challenge to the dominant class interests of the entire neighborhood. The land on which the settlement stands has been walled up by the KMDA to demonstrate its legal possession of the site, but no notice for eviction has yet been served (Roy, unpublished notes). Instead, notice boards have been put up by the Development Authority stating that the site is a BSUP project site meant for resettling the poor! It is important to mention that the Nonadanga residents did not seek any legal relief or ask for a stay order on the eviction. In the current situation, however, no one knows how long the residents will be able to resist the series of eviction drives that the government is obviously planning.

The time has come to decide whether the answer to this question will come from assertion at the institutional level or through social movements with support from a larger cross-section of society. The Nonadanga resistance of 2012 was supported by a large number of intellectuals, artists, writers, and professionals, in addition to several left and democratic-rights organizations that came forward to take part in the protest, assisted in bail formalities, and urged the government to discuss possibilities of resettlement for the residents. In the future, too, such support might be there. But it is important to understand that the right to the city is not just a right to urban space, it is also a right to work in the city. Fighting for the right to the city is thus part of a larger struggle that informal laborers and migrant workers are waging against neoliberal oppression that uses their cheap labor in all possible forms and simultaneously makes them more and more redundant in urban life and city planning. Actually, the entire community of Nonadanga belongs to this group and therefore participates in this dual struggle for which future support needs to be mobilized by concerned citizens. The struggle of Nonadanga and the other slum communities of Kolkata and elsewhere are all part of a larger struggle being waged against the neoliberal onslaught across the country. The question is whether it will be possible to link these struggles through collective effort based on an anticapitalist ideology and provide a wider arena of resistance at a macro level.

Terrains of Resistance

A proper understanding of the urban form of the transformative cities in India thus will remain superficial if it does not involve a discussion on the deepening polarization and disarticulation that the cities are experiencing and the people's resistance that arises out of these. Cities under neoliberal imposition not only concentrate a disproportionate share of corporate capital to become key sites for accumulation but also concentrate an increasingly large share of the disadvantaged and dispossessed (Sassen 1999). I have discussed how at various levels the current state power in India is turning out to be increasingly repressive by instituting deregulation norms and initiating change in the use-values of reconstructed spaces for the benefit of a narrower citizenry. The current urban restructuring in India, like in many other countries, is leading to increasing legitimization of the dispossession of the poor and to segregation of the city space and regulatory access to resources, which in turn are getting directly linked to the basic question of the "right to the city" and the right to make a livelihood according to the choice of the individual concerned. With large-scale stagnation and economic decline in villages, towns, and smaller cities in several parts of the country, large cities have become destinations for millions of poor migrants from across the country. With a shrunken organized sector and nonexpandable employment base, these cities, on the other hand, are no longer the centers of organized jobs they once were, nor are they able to productively absorb the migrants. In the given scenario of restructuring they are instead emerging as spaces of conflict and contradiction. The right to the city, in Indian cities in the present day, is getting linked to the right to livelihood, lending the urban social movements a distinct class content even if the latter are organized around the "travails of social reproduction" (Harvey 2012, 129).

The important question that needs to be raised here is whether the cities will become pivotal spaces for a new politics embedded in the counterclaims of the poor. Even though the claims of the corporate sector and the rich pave the way for a repressive and revanchist urbanism (Smith 1996), as evident from the consequences of urban redevelopment projects, the counterclaims made by the dispossessed struggling for entitlement and alternatives are impacting city life ever more than before. Although the patterns of claims reflect an overvalorized, powerful, small corporate center occupying an ever-expanding terrain and a devalorized periphery with a large number of people evidently marginalized, it goes without saying that the new politics of counterclaims and related struggles of the dispossessed will form the most solid part of neoliberal urbanism in India in the coming days. A wider mobilization of unorganized and temporary workers, household workers, and self-employed groups of different order—a result of the changing urban economies—is also showing up, which is making these struggles more effective. Harvey (2010) argues that the right to the city is something more than access to the city's resources; it is also the right to change the city according to the needs and desires of the larger section of the society. The above struggles are trying hard to be a part of that understanding with an aim to make cities socially just. But the fight needs to be carried out at two levels, as social justice is not always and only a product of militant movements (Fainstein 2003) and needs to be asserted in an aggressively contested institutional landscape too. To provide a wider arena in which subsequent struggles over cities will get articulated, struggles in each city need a backup of counterinstitutions to be developed by various other classes, capable of reframing issues in broad terms and mobilizing resources to fight for the aims of a larger section. In India, such multilevel struggles need to be organized in Kolkata, Mumbai, Delhi, Bangalore, Chennai, and many other large and small cities: by the urban poor, the Left, and democratic-rights organizations working together. Organizations like Lok Shakti Abhiyan, the Domestic Workers' Union, and the Garment Workers' Union, under the umbrella organization of the National Alliance of People's Movements (NAPM), are organizing struggles in several places. During the Nonadanga struggle, Delhi Krantikari Naujawan Sabha, the People's Union of Democratic Rights, Delhi Metro Kamgar Union, the Democratic Students' Union, the Jamia Teachers' Solidarity Forum, Posco Pratirodh Solidarity, and several other groups from Delhi, the Mumbai chapter of NAPM, and many other groups came out in support. The need of the hour is to coordinate these groups, to coordinate the dual struggles fought at institutional and noninstitutional levels in a number of locations.

This brings us to the final issue of the nature of urban social movements and movements launched at a wider level across the country, and the necessity to link them through an anticapitalist political ideology. Cases of land appropriation, displacement, and socioeconomic dispossession for the facilitation of globally oriented activities have not only become innumerable, they are uniformly affecting urban as well as rural areas, and with the same intensity. The magnitude and the form of displacement no doubt vary from place to place depending on the nature of the "activity," but the vulnerability of the affected population, which constitutes a huge proportion of the total population of cities, villages, and forests, is everywhere on the rise (Action Aid 2008). Let us take a few recent cases. In the state of Chhattisgarh, the Kelu River has been forcibly handed over to industry; construction of a private dam on the Kurkut River in the same state has deprived the local community of its age-long access to the river; systematic evictions of slum dwellers are taking place in several areas of Mumbai (Agarwadi, Govandi, Bandra, and Santacruz), Delhi (Noida, Greater Noida), and Kolkata (Rajarhat, Nonadanga, Jadavpur), while resistance has been met with brutal police atrocity;

the struggle for justice in several villages in Orissa against land appropriation for SEZs and corporate mining has been systematically suppressed by state violence; besides the cases of displacement of the above kind, in Chhattisgarh and Madhya Pradesh alone hundreds of villages have been relocated in order to make army camps, air force bases, and wildlife sanctuaries; in an ecologically and geologically fragile region of northeast India, on the Brahmaputra and Barak River basins, the central government is constructing 168 dams to supply electricity to large cities in southern and northern India, which will not only be of no use to the people of the region (Vagholikar and Das 2010) but will lead to tremendous ecological instability. All these actions are making each segment of space in the country political and contradictory. Resistance struggles of diverse forms erupting in different parts of the county (Banerjee-Guha 2013a) are consequences of the above.

Taking place at various scales, these movements are essentially questioning the current development path of the country. Many of these movements, except the Maoist-led armed resistance organized in the tribal areas of several states against corporate takeover, are nonviolent mass movements. Many, as well, are not organized on socialist ideals. But almost all, in one way or another, are challenging the anti-people policies of the state and exposing entrenched power relations at multiple levels. When led by groups other than those of the left, the movements do not have a focus on class; they remain embedded in the struggles of daily life, where they may prove significant in reconstructing the "everyday" space between the state and society. For the same reason, however, despite taking positions against the day-to-day exploitation they experience, they do not always go on to direct themselves against the political-economic nexus responsible for the exploitation. The political ideology behind these movements often remains fuzzy and the direction of their struggles unfocused. As the forces against which these struggles are aimed are partners on the neoliberal front, it becomes imperative to link them through a strong anticapitalist ideology in order to carve out an innovative path toward social transformation, failing which they may become vulnerable to the forces of exclusionary politics or the co-opting strategies of institutional power structures at various levels (Banerjee-Guha 2013b).

Neoliberal capitalist exploitation is a multifaceted phenomenon. Millions are being uprooted from villages, towns, and cities across the country to make space for gigantic projects like SEZs, private cities, urban infrastructures, upscale ports, corporate mining, or nuclear projects. At the same time, by the same process, these uprooted people are being converted into cheap labor in corporate units or in the same projects that uprooted them. This is not just happening in India: The scenario is the same in many other countries, like China, Bangladesh, Malaysia, and Australia. The uprooted people work for miserably low wages, much lower than government-specified minimum wage levels. They work overtime, often without extra pay, and most of the time their entire family works, including the children and the elderly, to make ends meet. The neoliberal-capitalist demand for time impinges on their personal and biological needs and makes sure that they do not have any space for themselves, any opportunity to spend time with other workers, or any chance to engage in discussion and mobilize for protest. It is therefore necessary that they develop a clear idea about the forces that make this globally structured exploitation possible, no matter where it takes place or in what form.

This is a formidable theoretical and practical task for the Left in India. The struggles that are being launched across the country are genuinely important, because they are bringing out the patterns of space-specific exploitations and thereby opening up possibilities for challenging the global-local nexus of capitalist power once they get interlinked with each other. And now that the nature of the working class has changed, the organized factories have been largely dismantled, and the dynamics of class exploitation have gone beyond the workplace, there is no reason why one should not consider the possibility of launching a class struggle and a struggle for citizenship rights together (Harvey 2012, 128–29). The movements launched all over the country against dispossession, marginalization, and denial of basic rights are symptoms of the total restructuring of the socioeconomic space on the basis of dispossession and predatory practices. Denial of the workers' right to land and livelihood in villages and cities, denial of the indigenous people's right to resources and community-oriented economic life in the forests of Orissa, Madhya Pradesh, Chhattisgarh, Bastar, and Jharkhand, and denial of the right to self-determination in Kashmir and Nagaland are all cases in point. The terrains of dispossession are complex, but they are seamless. And that makes it an urgent need to look again at the old ideas of class struggle and mass movements. As it would be both naive and dangerous to celebrate all forms of resistance (Banerjee 2012), it would also be wrong to ignore the possibility of many movements that, once coalesced, can emerge as a formidable platform for larger anticapitalist struggles. The task lies there: in analyzing the movements, humanizing the strategy and tactics, invigorating them with an anticapitalist ideological base, and facilitating their coming together. This will take the fight for the right to the city beyond its limits, to a wider level. Hope lies there too.

The author thanks Partho Sarathi Ray and other members of Sanhati, Kolkata, for sharing the day-to-day details of the movement in Nonadanga.

Above, a resident of Nonadanga sitting on the spot where her house used to stand before demolition; *below*, protest march organized by the Committee against Demolition.

Above, Nonadanga being bulldozed; *below*, post-demolition efforts to restart life. The struggle is led by the Committee against Demolition. *Facing page*: "State bulldozes Nonadanga Slum. Voice your protest. Support the just demand for rehabilitation.
—Committee against Demolition"

সরকারী বুলডোজারে গুঁড়িয়ে গেল নোনাডাঙার বস্তিবাসীদের ঘর।

প্রতিবাদে সোচ্চার হোন।
যথাযথ পুনর্বাসনের দাবীতে
আন্দোলনের পাশে দাঁড়ান।

উচ্ছেদ প্রতিরোধ কমিটি

উচ্ছেদ প্রতিরোধ কমিটির পক্ষে উজ্জ্বল সাহা (৯৭৪৮৯২৪২৪২), নোনাডাঙা মজদুর পল্লী কর্তৃক প্রকাশিত।

Chapter 8

The Struggle of the Urban Poor against Forced Eviction in Jakarta

Muhammad Ridha

F
orced eviction seems inseparable from the development of contemporary cities. Each year, hundreds of thousands of urban dwellers are displaced from their homes and livelihoods in cities around the world. As the number of people living in poverty has risen from 17% to 28% in the last ten years (Haddad 2012), forced eviction has come to seem desirable as an attempt to take more control over urban development through the construction of infrastructure (lights, roads, sewage) and services (health and education). The existence of the urban poor only creates slums and untidiness within a city. Forced eviction is thus a necessary foundation for modernization. Rapid modernization of the city not only enables urban progress, it also brings fundamental changes for the inhabitants when the traditional rule over land is diminished and replaced by a more refined legal system, which will make city governance easier and simpler. Ultimately, the argument goes, forced eviction is beneficial for all the city's inhabitants.

Optimistic as it is, this view seems to neglect the real process of the city itself. As Davis (2006) warned, the current form of the urban process has created a discriminatory city and could potentially lead to its own destruction. While cities have been able to construct many skyscrapers indicating abundance of wealth, the working and lower-middle classes still live in overcrowded, poor, or informal housing, have inadequate access to safe water and sanitation, and are in constant threat of losing their shelter (Davis 2004, 13). Therefore, urban development has been informed by the massive marginalization and segregation of certain classes in order to promote progress, beautification, and even social justice. The poor must withdraw from the urban space for the advantage of landowners, foreign investors, elite homeowners, and middle-class commuters (Davis 2006, 98). One logical implication that might follow from this process is that rampant poverty can be a fertile ground for the emergence of reactionary consciousness among the urban poor. In his survey of fourteen countries representing 62% of the world's Muslim population, Mousseau (2011) has found that rather than religious factors, urban poverty might be the main determinant for the emergence of Islamist terror. This finding strengthens the thesis that terrorist groups are likely to obtain support and recruits from among the urban poor by pursuing their economic interests in society, which should make us at least reflect on how rampant marginalization of the urban poor can create counterresponses that might threaten the whole urban process.

With the above situation as background, this essay tries to elaborate on different processes that involve marginalization of the urban poor in which the bleak picture above does not represent the only possible outcome. The urban poor can emerge as a potential source of agency for better conditions in the city itself. Instead of assuming that the urban poor will always be a threat to the city's development, I argue that the presence of the urban poor enables different development processes. The orientation of municipal authorities toward economic growth often becomes the main impetus for forced eviction as the manifestation of the marginalization of the urban poor. However, the urban poor, through their struggle against forced evictions, are capable of challenging this status quo to reshape conditions in the city and the urban regime ruling it. The collectivity of the urban poor through organization and self-education will be the crucial instrument for constructing the new urban process.

The Making of the Urban Poor

The existence of Jakarta's urban poor cannot be separated from the dynamics of Indonesia's political economy as a whole. Economic liberalization encouraged by neoliberalism enables unequal development from which the urban poor emerge as a class. After the fall of the New Order regime of President Suharto, which had lasted over thirty years from the late 1960s to 1998, Indonesia had to rearrange its economic structure to fit the interests of the international market. It integrated the domestic market with the global market. The neoliberalization of Indonesia's economy cannot be separated from the imposition of the structural adjustment program of the International Monetary Fund, which forces the government of Indonesia to liberalize and deregulate.

In the era of neoliberal globalization, Indonesia achieved a high rate of economic growth through this process, reaching 6.5% in 2011: one of the highest rates in the global economy. The case of economic growth in Indonesia illuminates the neoliberal globalization process of accumulation by dispossession. This can be understood as a process of accumulating capital by dispossessing people, through coercion, of what they own and what they already have as their right, as part of embedding capitalist relations of production (Harvey 2003). It is noticeable that Indonesia's economic growth correlated with the proliferation of coercion by the state apparatus. Neoliberal globalization thus generated fertile ground for the impoverishment of Indonesia's population.

There are two modes of accumulation that lead to impoverishment within the process of economic growth. The first is the massive extraction of natural resources to be sold on the international market; the second is the exploitation of human resources as cheap labor. This exploitation has given Indonesia significant trade surplus, which helped boost the economic growth rate to 3.3% in the third quarter of 2011, according to data released by the Central Statistical Bureau on January 7, 2012.

Although Indonesia is still exporting oil, the amount of oil and gas exports is relatively small when compared with the value of non-oil exports. According to the Indonesian Ministry of Trade (Karina 2012), the contribution of the non-oil export industry was 61% of total exports in 2011. According to a report released by Bank Indonesia, there were three main commodities that contributed greatly to the value of exported goods: coal (15.5%), palm oil (10.2%), and rubber (9.1%). Interestingly, these are all commodities from extraction industries that depend on the exploitation of natural resources. These data indicate that Indonesia's economy is being organized under a global division of labor in which Indonesia is no longer a commodity-producing country adding value (for example, through industrial manufacturing) but rather a raw-material supplier.

This economic structure facilitates the first mode of accumulation: exploiting natural resources. Land ownership in Indonesia must now be restructured to meet the demands of global capitalism for raw materials. The restructuring generates the proliferation of land grabbing that leads to agrarian conflicts in the country. The Consortium for Agrarian Reform has shown that in 2011 there were 163 agrarian conflicts in Indonesia with 22 casualties. These agrarian conflicts involved 69,975 families and the area of disputed land reached 472,048 hectares. Of these 163 agrarian conflicts, 97 cases occurred in the plantation sector, 36 cases in the forestry sector, 21 cases in the infrastructure sector, 8 cases in mining, and one in a coastal area. Most of the conflicts involved violent acts by the state apparatus to preserve the interests of corporations against the communities. Therefore, it can be said that the integration of Indonesia's economy exacerbates agrarian conflicts because of global capital's demand to control space within Indonesia's territory to satisfy global consumption.

The land grabbing has led to the expulsion of the productive forces from their space of production. This process enables a proletarianization of the rural population in which they become "free" labor and therefore migrate to urban areas. However, the proletarianization does not necessarily mean they enter production relations in the city. They may fail to find employment altogether or become engaged in the informal sector; in either case, they remain excluded from the set of formal production relations that constitute local and global capitalism. The structure of employment is currently dominated by informal workers, who make up 63% of the whole workforce in Indonesia (Ahniar and Akbar, 2012).

This employment structure becomes the foundation of impoverishment and the emergence of the urban poor. The urban poor in Jakarta usually operate in the informal sector. It is common for them to have nonpermanent jobs or to be engaged in the small business sector. They usually run their businesses in public space, for instance as street vendors. Unfortunately, commercial activity is forbidden in most public space. This then makes the urban poor vulnerable to harassment by the police and up to sixty days' imprisonment.

Another process that accounts for the emergence of the urban poor in Jakarta is low wages. The high rate of unemployment and the proliferation of informal-sector work leads to further impoverishment of the population. Economically, high unemployment means a large supply of available labor, which drives down wage rates. This structure means Indonesia has the lowest minimum wage in Southeast Asia. On average, Indonesia's minimum wage reaches only US$0.06 an hour, lower than those of Malaysia (US$2.88), Thailand (US$1.63), and the Philippines (US$1.04) (Asia Monitor Resource Center 2012, 45). Data on the consumer price index and the average monthly wages of industrial workers from 2007 to 2011 show that despite increases in the nominal wage rate, real wages in Indonesia have stagnated or even fallen. From 2007 until September 2011, the increase of nominal wages did not keep up with increases in the consumer price index. From 2007 to 2008, real wages fell from Rp 1,019,000 to Rp 969,100. This loss was recovered in June 2010 and real wages even went up in September 2010, reaching Rp 1,125,200. Nonetheless, they fell again in the following quarter, and by September 2011 the real wages of workers amounted to only Rp 1,041,200. So in spite of periodic fluctuations, there is stagnation in the overall rate of real wages.

The Growth Machine and Forced Evictions in Jakarta

To understand forced evictions against Jakarta's urban poor, it is necessary to highlight the development of Jakarta itself, which enables this process. As the capital of Indonesia, Jakarta is the epicenter of the country's economic growth. According to official statistics, Jakarta alone contributed 16.46% of economic growth in 2014. This is the highest contribution among all Indonesian provinces.

The significance of Jakarta in Indonesia's economy cannot be separated from the historical experience of uneven development at the state level. In the era of the New Order regime (1965–1997), the economy was highly centralized on Java, with Jakarta as its main city. This arrangement was a deliberate attempt to strengthen the political grip of the central government on the local authorities. The centralization of power enabled centralization of the economy, which accelerated Jakarta's development, transforming it into a city with one of the highest new building development rates in the world (Puspaningtyas 2014).

Between 2013 and 2014, property growth reached 20–30% annually. Although in 2015 it was estimated to be slowing, the rate of growth still stood around 10–15%. According to Bank Indonesia, in 2015 there were new commercial developments under way, like the malls in Lippo Puri and Pantai Indah Kapuk, along with a number of residential developments such as TBS Linera Apartment Services, Fraser Place Setiabudi Sky Garden, Pejaten Park Residence, and Fraser Suite Ciputra World (Bank Indonesia 2015).

This growth is related to the increasing demand for property consumption. This can be seen from the trend of commercial property rental in the second quarter of 2015. For instance, occupancy has increased from 96.90% to 97.34% for retail spaces, 81.33% to 88.11% for apartments, 68.22% to 79.8% for convention halls, and 54.04% to 59.99% for luxury hotels. Within the same period, the sales rate of commercial property also rose significantly.

Here one needs to ask an important question: what is the social basis for promoting and supporting this kind of urban growth? An insight developed by Logan and Molotch (1987) can be useful to understanding this process. They called this form of social relation a "growth machine" in which the economic growth of the city (and its spatial development) is sustained by the power of some sector of the capitalist class: in this case, the developers and rentiers who profit from urban investment and development. Therefore, the growth of the city not only in economic but also physical terms is facilitated by the power of the rentiers. This sector of the capitalist class operates through forging social alliances with several groups within the government and society who also benefit from the city's growth. For the government, the city's growth can be used for sustaining legitimacy, since it can also generate government income and political support.

Harding (1995) argued that there are three forms of social alliances that construct the growth machine. First, the developers, financiers, and those who directly benefit from the development process; second, social groups that benefit indirectly, usually by the increased use of products and services due to the development process, like local media and materials suppliers for the developers; and third, any interest groups in the society that also benefit from the economic growth in the city. The interactions between these alliances enable a sort of network of interest in the urban process. Their activity becomes the structure of the growth machine in the city that consequently promotes development and contestation over the urban space.

Significantly, urban development is not necessarily produced by urban planning but by the political (and economic) struggle within and among these alliances. Jakarta's development proves this thesis. This can be seen in how by big property developers and conglomerates promote the development of property. Urban development in Jakarta is dominated by the interests of big businesses and designed in accordance with their interests rather than through democratic planning by the citizens. Indeed, violation of land use statutes becomes common in the process of development. For example, water absorption areas in Kelapa Gading and Sunter have been converted into commercial complexes; several urban forests in Senayan, Tomang, and Kapuk are undergoing a similar process.

This condition generates spatial contradiction in Jakarta. The contradiction lies in the spatial process of Jakarta's importance in economic growth as opposed to the social needs of its inhabitants, who define the urban space as a space for living. Land tenure in Jakarta operates under a logic of speculation in which its value often experiences excessive price increases. This marginalizes some sectors of Jakarta's population, especially the urban poor, from the urban process. Due to their economic condition, the urban poor are rarely entitled to land tenure, since they cannot afford it.

This forces the urban poor to find their own solutions to be able to live in Jakarta. As part of their survival, many occupy idle lands. However, this becomes a problem for the government since the land is already owned, and thus the poor are occupying it illegally. The government usually one-sidedly deems the vacant land occupied by the urban poor as unfit for habitation, which enables the policy of forced evictions against the urban poor.

Interestingly, most of the forced evictions have been related to infrastructural projects. The Legal Aid Institute of Jakarta has documented thirty cases of forced evictions in 2015, most of them related to the infrastructural development of reservoirs, normalization of the riverbanks, construction of city parks and railways, and toll road projects. These projects are supported by Jakarta's government. From 2009, infrastructural development has become the main expenditure of the city's budget. Therefore, the forced evictions are funded under infrastructural budgeting. In 2014, the city administration of Jakarta allocated a public budget of Rp 6 trillion for fighting "illegal settlements."

Ananta (2015) has argued that this pattern is related, again, to the interests of the "growth machine" alliance. In this case, eviction in Jakarta not only is an attempt to contain the negative effects of economic growth but also serves a positive function in an economic growth model with infrastructure development as its backbone. This functionality arises when the development of infrastructure involves a developer class as its main actor. Public funds are allocated to the development corporation to run infrastructural development projects and thus increase its profits. This mode of local government resource allocation is distinctly beneficial to the urban developer.

Jakarta's Urban Poor Struggle against Forced Eviction

The struggle of Jakarta's urban poor against forced evictions is related to their concrete experience with the development of the city. The 1997 economic crisis was an important juncture in their lives in Jakarta. The terrible impact of the crisis led to an increase of collective action. The urban poor reclaimed hectares of abandoned and idle land owned by companies or private entities for resettlement or for their agricultural activities. People were also allowed to conduct informal economic activities in several public spaces in Jakarta. These activities were in a sense inevitable, since the idle land was a rare economic opportunity for the urban poor who suffered severely from the economic difficulties. From 1998 until 2001, evictions essentially stopped. The authorities in Jakarta at that time had no choice but to tolerate such activities. In 1998, Jakarta's authorities even promoted allowing poor people to use idle land owned by the government as a matter of policy. However, the situation changed dramatically when Indonesia experienced economic recovery. In 2001, a wave of forced evictions began.

Interestingly, despite an aggressive campaign of forced evictions on the part of the authorities, Jakarta's urban poor did not become passive victims. Although on the structural level forced evictions seemed to go unchallenged, at a micro level the process occurred in dynamic form, and many attempts at eviction were met with resistance. The urban poor transformed themselves into active subjects of resistance.

This can be seen in how the urban poor organized themselves, establishing community organizations to unite them and strengthen their fight against eviction. The need to strengthen their bargaining power against the authorities was the main impetus for Jakarta's urban poor to develop their own organization. Take for example the experience of Pesatuan Rakyat Tergusur, the Union of Evicted People (PRT), one of the urban-poor organizations active against forced evictions. The organization was established in response to an eviction in Jembatan Besi, Tambora, West Jakarta, in 2002. Those who lived in Jembatan Besi were accused of illegal settlement and thus violating public order; the government decided to evict them to restore the land. However, the settlers saw the government decision as arbitrary. They felt that the land, although illegally inhabited, had been maintained and cultivated by them, which gave them a right to it. Ignoring this fact was an injustice, since in maintaining the land they had contributed to the urban process itself.

To deal with the evictions, the aim of PRT was to maintain the right of the urban poor to live in Jembatan Besi or else to get decent compensation from the government to make sure they would be able to resettle in different places. Since the government saw these demands as invalid due to the illegal status of the petitioners, the execution of eviction orders was unavoidable. Responding to this situation, the first thing PRT did was try to use its lobbying capacity to discourage the government's plans, making use of its resources and network to engage in dialogue with officials and persuade them to cancel the eviction. To some extent, they even tried a win-win solution in which they would agree to be evicted on the condition that they would receive decent compensation. Nevertheless, the process was only effective as a stalling tactic. The government intended to carry out its decision by any means necessary, even the use of force. Yet when the evicted were faced with coercive acts, they usually responded with readiness to fight back against the violence.

The preparation of the urban poor to deal with state violence had always been accompanied by collective efforts to educate themselves. Self-education was crucial, since resistance against the violence of the state required a sense of conviction, a consciousness that what they were about to do was right and noble: that the urban poor in fact have the right to decent lives and that this right should be guaranteed by the state. The process of self-education was conducted collectively: the first thing they did was to hold a public gathering around the eviction area as an attempt to bring their cause to a broader audience. In the public gathering, all members of the organization were allowed to express and share their thoughts and experiences regarding the eviction process. They invited mass media to cover their struggle and several other civil society organizations to come and show solidarity with the urban poor. After the public gathering, they held a mass demonstration protesting the local government institution that was failing to guarantee the right of the poor to live in Jakarta. When their aspirations were ignored, they proceeded with a hunger strike. While on strike, they filed a case with the National Commission for Human Rights to complain about the human rights violation behind the government's decision of forced eviction. Physical clashes between the PRT and the authorities would take place only if all previous attempts to make the government cancel the evictions had failed.

The experience of PRT cannot be generalized as the only form, or even best practice, of struggle against forced eviction for the urban poor. The PRT's struggle lasted only a month. In the end Jembatan Besi was "successfully cleaned." To all appearances, Jakarta is still a city dominated by the power of capital and directing systematic discrimination against its citizens, especially the urban poor (see Wilson 2015). However, what I want to highlight from their experience is how even the urban poor have the capacity to exercise agency and therefore power. Several important dimensions of the struggle—such as building an organization as a main instrument of resistance, self-education, and the readiness to be combative against state violence—affected the attitude of the urban regime in Jakarta. The authorities became more sensitive to demands for compensation. As Dika Muhamad, an activist in Jakarta, told me in December 2015, the government changed its approach to persuading the urban poor to leave their settlements in the decade following these incidents. They started to provide new residences for the evictees in public apartments. Although most of those apartments could not be considered as decent and meeting basic standards, it was undoubtedly the struggle of the urban poor that played the crucial role in changing how the urban regime dealt with them.

The shift in the urban regime's approach toward the urban poor was also related to the democratization of Indonesian politics after the 1998 Reformasi, which changed the contours of the political process in Jakarta. After the implementation of decentralization in Indonesia, Jakarta's citizens were allowed to directly elect their governor. This enabled the urban political structure to become responsive to social dynamics, including social unrest. Any social conflict that occurs in Jakarta now influences the political process, as members of the local political elite will try to capture this condition for gaining political support. The ruling class needs support from the citizens in order to sustain its legitimacy in the eyes of the people.

So it was a combination of democratization at the local level with the struggle of the urban poor that shaped political change in Jakarta. While, as argued before, Jakarta's regime is still making economic growth through infrastructure the main public spending priority, the government has started to recognize the social needs of Jakarta's population. For example, social spending on health and education has gained a place among the public-spending priorities. In 2013, spending on health even became the government's top priority (Ananta 2015). Although the delivery of health services is still problematic and riddled with corruption, this change at least indicates a shift of attention within the urban regime.

Not only did the struggle of the urban poor change the situation around them, it also changed how the urban poor are seeing themselves. As Muhamad went on to explain (personal communication, December 13, 2015), the experience of struggling against forced eviction enabled a new politicization of the urban poor. Where once they might have seen themselves as merely helpless and dispossessed, the struggle led them to the construction of themselves as citizens of Jakarta. The process of education that took place during the evictions, initially conducted as a way of convincing themselves to defend their own lives against state brutality, introduced them to the idea of their rights as citizens. The struggling urban poor started to absorb the idea that since they were also citizens in the city, their lives should be guaranteed and protected by the state. Interestingly, this politicization allowed them to engage more readily with broader issues of social welfare. When the urban poor become involved in activism, their struggle usually centers on demands for the government to guarantee the basic needs of citizens. According to Muhamad, this gives their struggle a unique and important position in relation to the struggles of other sectors of the working class in Indonesia, such as the labor or peasant movements. If labor and peasant movements are usually engaged in the struggle to fulfill their normative rights as laborers or peasants (wages, land, and so on), the urban poor movement struggles to guarantee more universal rights: basic citizens' rights. It can be argued that the opportunity for direct confrontation between the urban poor and the state apparatus shapes the form of this struggle.

Lessons Learned

What lessons can be learned from the struggle experience of the urban poor of Jakarta? First, the concrete struggle of the urban poor can contribute to shaping the urban process. In this case, the city should be understood as a container within which the dynamics of social relations operate. Social forces inherently situated in the context of the city's development are not insulated in a vacuum; they are always interacting in complex ways. Capital may dominate as the main force in the city's development, but the marginalization that occurs in the process also "elevates" the position of the urban poor. Initially, they respond with basic attempts to survive in the urban space, but the moment they decide to become actively engaged in the struggle against forced eviction, they are able to exercise agency. This feature should not be underestimated if one wants to understand the development of the city and the urban process surrounding it.

Another interesting lesson is the emergence of what Raymond Williams calls "militant particularism," which is a process of "the unique and extraordinary character of working-class self-organization . . . [trying] to connect particular struggle to general struggle in one quite special way. It has set out, as a movement, to make real what is at first sight the extraordinary claim that the defense and advancement of certain particular interests, properly brought together, are in fact the general interest" (Williams, quoted in Harvey 1996, 32). As I have argued, the concrete struggle of the urban poor in Jakarta, initially aimed at protecting their particular livelihood, has been able to transform itself into a struggle for the rights of citizens. As the urban poor try to win their cause, they inevitably need to gain support from society. In this case, rather than seeing their struggle as alien, they needed to reframe it as being inherently in the interests of Jakarta's citizenry as a whole. This discursive dynamic led to the politicization of the urban poor as citizens of Jakarta.

Strikingly, the politicization of the urban poor was also facilitated by the politicization of the city itself. The close alliance between the interests of the state and the interests of capital in achieving economic growth has led the city to become the site of political struggle. The vulgar manifestation of economic growth that only benefits a handful of social groups generates conditions of marginalization and oppression for many inhabitants of the city. As Miller and Nicholls (2013, 458) argue, the discriminatory process that occurs in the city is enabling social formations that might challenge the oppression: "Encountering denigrating limitations in everyday life is essential to the process of group politicization, driven by the sharp disconnect between a group's expectations of equal rights and treatment, and everyday experiences that violate those expectations. The city, in this sense, becomes the frontline space where inequality and injustice are experienced. When groups become politically conscious and can mobilize sufficient resources, their first political targets tend to be those urban policies and practices that restricted their civil or political rights."

Therefore, politicization within the struggle of the urban poor answers an important question about the relationship between the state and broader societal forces. Rather than being an autonomous entity outside the society, the state operating in the city is strongly determined by its social needs and antagonisms. Poulantzas (1980) argues that the state should be understood as relational rather than static, because class struggle is effectively present in the physical space of the state apparatus. The state is not a direct determination of class power but a condensation of material relationships of force determined by class struggle. Consequently, it can be said that the state is a locus for the collision and contestation of power—which means that it is not simply determined by market forces. This means there is no deterministic outcome in the relation between the state and capital. Jessop (1990) adds an important insight, arguing that this nondeterministic relation is a strategic one. By "strategic," he means a system whose structure and operation are more accessible to some forms of political strategy than others. Thus some types of state policy will be more open to the influence of social forces than others, depending on the strategies adopted to gain state power.

Nevertheless, the struggle of the urban poor is best defined as what Bayat (1997, 5) calls "the quiet encroachment of the ordinary," meaning that "quiet practices by the very ordinary and often silent people engender significant social changes." Although the direct confrontation conducted by the urban poor during the evictions did not necessarily result in victory or any tangible gain, their concrete experience of resisting state power influenced the political process that took place in the city itself. There might be no major structural change within the city's formal process, but as I have argued, the combativeness of the urban poor when challenging measures that ran against their interest pressured the authorities to become more lenient. The city authorities, whether they want to or not, must take into account the demand of the urban poor to live humanely in the city.

Above: A mass rally of trade union and urban poor activists against the free trade agreement in Southeast Asia and various government policies takes place May 1, 2015, on Jl. M. H. Thamrin thoroughfare in central Jakarta. *Below*: Urban poor activists demand that the government of Jakarta provide holiday allowance for Idul Fitri festivities, July 1, 2015, in front of the Ministry of Social Affairs of the Republic of Indonesia. (All photos for this chapter by Mark Philip Stadler.)

Above: Urban poor and activists demand the provision of social welfare for poor families in Jakarta, February 6, 2015, at the Social Services Department. *Below*: An activist delivers a speech on the same occasion.

Contributor Biographies

Trevor Ngwane

Trevor Ngwane is a scholar-activist who has over the years devoted as much time to academic work as to community and political activism. He studied at the University of Fort Hare during the apartheid days for four years and did not graduate due to various "student disturbances." He obtained his BA (sociology and psychology) degree through the University of South Africa and his BA Honours (sociology) at the University of the Witwatersrand. For two decades he has been active in trade unions, social movements, and political organizations as an organizer and militant, a period that has spanned the transition from apartheid to a democratic society. He is also involved in international movements for social and economic justice and was active for several years in the African Social Forum, a component of the World Social Forum. In 2011 he obtained his MA at the University of KwaZulu-Natal's School of Development Studies and is currently reading for a PhD at the University of Johannesburg, where he is attached to the Research Chair in Social Change and works as a researcher in the Rebellion of the Poor protest-monitoring and database-compilation project. Ngwane is currently active in the Socialist Group, Democratic Left Front, and United Front, organizations that seek a pro-working-class, pro-poor future for South Africa and the world. He lives in Soweto, Johannesburg. Email: trevorngwane@gmail.com.

Luke Sinwell

Luke Sinwell, who earned his PhD at Witwatersrand University in Johannesburg, South Africa, is currently a senior researcher with the South African Research Chair in Social Change at the University of Johannesburg. His research interests include the politics and conceptualization of participatory development and governance, social movements and housing struggles, direct action as a method to transform power relations, ethnographic research methods, and action research.

He is the author of *The Spirit of Marikana: The Rise of Insurgent Trade Unionism in South Africa*. In addition he has published in many academic journals and authored chapters in academic books. Sinwell is a coauthor of *Marikana: A View from the Mountain and a Case to Answer* (Jacana, 2012; Ohio University Press, 2013) and the coeditor of *Contesting Transformation: Popular Resistance in Twenty-First Century South Africa* (Pluto Press, 2012). Email: lsinwell@uj.ac.za.

Immanuel Ness

Immanuel Ness is a professor of political science at Brooklyn College of the City University of New York and a senior research associate at the University of Johannesburg. His research focuses on working-class mobilization, trade unions, socialist political movements, workers in the Global South, migration, resistance, and social movements. Ness is author of *Southern Insurgency: The Coming of the Global Working Class* (Pluto Press, 2015), *Guest Workers and Resistance to US Corporate Despotism* (University of Illinois Press, 2011), and *Immigrants, Unions, and the U.S. Labor Market* (Temple University Press, 2005). He is general editor, with Peter Bellwood, of *The Encyclopedia of Global Human Migration* (Wiley, 2013). He is finishing a book on migration and inequality in the Global South. Ness is editor of *New Forms of Worker Organization* (PM Press, 2014) and coeditor with Dario Azzellini of *Ours to Master and to Own: Worker Control from the Commune to the Present* (Haymarket Books, 2011). He is editor of the peer-reviewed quarterly *Journal of Labor and Society*. Email: iness@brooklyn.cuny.edu.

Ayokunle Olumuyiwa Omobowale

Ayokunle Olumuyiwa Omobowale holds a PhD in sociology from the University of Ibadan. Ayokunle's doctoral research was on political clientelism and rural development in selected communities in Ibadan, Nigeria. He studies African-development, cultural, rural, political, and urban issues contextually. He is a recipient of the Ibadan University Postgraduate School Award for scholarly publication (2007), the IFRA (French Institute for Research in Africa) Research Fellowship (2009), and the American Council of Learned Societies–African Humanities Programme Post-doctoral Fellowship (2010), and he has been an African Studies Association Presidential Fellow (2014). Dr. Omobowale was also a visiting scholar at the Center for African Studies at Rutgers University in November 2014 and currently teaches sociology at the University of Ibadan, Nigeria. He served on the board of editors of the *International Encyclopaedia of Revolution and Protest* (Wiley-Blackwell, 2009). His recent research includes "Peripheral Scholarship and the Context of Foreign Paid Publishing in Nigeria" (*Current Sociology*, 2014), "An Ethnographic Textual Analysis of Aging and the Elders in South Western Nigeria" (*Canadian Journal of Sociology*, 2014), and "Stories of the 'Dark' Continent: Crude Constructions, Diasporic Identity, and International Aid to Africa" (*International Sociology*, 2015). He is the author of *The Tokunbo Phenomenon and the Second-Hand Economy in Nigeria* (Peter Lang, 2013).

Adefemi Abdulmojeed Adeyanju

Adefemi Abdulmojeed Adeyanju holds a BSc Honours degree in sociology from the University of Ibadan, Nigeria, and a diploma in accounting. He has gained professional experience in banking and electoral services. Adefemi is committed to community service and livelihood enhancements in slums.

Swapna Banerjee-Guha

Swapna Banerjee-Guha, currently Senior Fellow of the Indian Council of Social Science Research, was formerly a professor of Development Studies at the Tata Institute of Social Sciences (TISS), Mumbai. Prior to joining TISS she was professor and chair of Human Geography at the University of Mumbai for several years. She received her initial training in human geography at Presidency College and the University of Calcutta, where she received her doctoral degree in the mid-1970s, and subsequently started her teaching career at Burdwan University in West Bengal. A postdoctoral Fulbright Fellow at Johns Hopkins University in the mid-1980s, Banerjee-Guha has taught and researched at institutions in North America, England, Europe, and Asia, and was a member of the steering committee of the International Critical Geography Group. She has served on the editorial boards of several national and international journals and is currently the South Asia editor of the journal *Human Geography*. A pioneer in the field of critical social science research in India, she has pursued her academic work throughout while remaining linked with political activism. She is a recipient of the Quality of Life Award of the Association of Commonwealth Universities for her contributions to development research in South Asia. Banerjee-Guha is a bilingual author and translator, writing in both English and Bengali.

Simone da Silva Ribeiro Gomes

Simone da Silva Ribeiro Gomes holds a PhD in sociology at IESP (Instituto de Estudos Sociais e Políticos), Rio de Janeiro State University, Brazil. Her research and publications center on political socialization, social movements, political violence, drug trafficking, and coercive environments for collective action in Latin America. She has been an activist researcher in urban and feminist social movements in Brazil and France.

Patrick O'Hare

Patrick O'Hare is an Economic and Social Research Council–funded PhD candidate in social anthropology at the University of Cambridge. He has conducted fieldwork in Argentina and Uruguay with both informal- and formal-sector recycling workers and studies the politics and economics of waste. He is interested in the study of nonconventional labor organization, post-neoliberalism, waste, and landfill economies. Patrick has long been involved in radical activism, including pro-independence Scottish politics, solidarity activity with Palestinian and Arab peoples, and the student movement, including a spell as president of the University of St Andrews Students' Association. He has recently become the proud father of a beautiful wee girl.

Muhammad Ridha

Muhammad Ridha is a scholar-activist heavily involved with the working-class movement in Indonesia. After finishing his bachelor's degree in political science at the University of Indonesia in 2008, Ridha continued his studies at Murdoch University in Australia, where he earned his master's degree in Development Studies in 2015 with a thesis entitled "The Development of Universal Social Security in Indonesia." He is also active in the Working People's Party (Partai Rakyat Pekerja) and currently serves as the regional secretary of Jakarta's Confederation of Indonesian People's Movements (Konfederasi Pergerakan Rakyat Indonesia), a cross-class mass organization. He is also a member of the editorial board of indoprogress.com, an educational website aimed at disseminating progressive and pro-working-class ideas in Indonesia. Aside from his activism, he is also engaged with the research activity of the Research Center for Crisis and Alternative Development Strategy and the Center for Political Studies (Pusat Kajian Politik), University of Indonesia. His research interests encompass political economy, urban politics, public policy, and contemporary political theory.

Claudia Delgado Villegas

Claudia Delgado Villegas holds a PhD from Rutgers University. She did her undergraduate studies at the Universidad Nacional Autónoma de México (UNAM). She has been a lecturer at Rutgers, the City University of New York, Seton Hall University, and UNAM. Her research topics include social movements, Mexican migration to the United States, socio-spatial inequality in the contemporary city, and visual methodologies for social research. She has collaborated with the Center for Research and Higher Studies in Social Anthropology in Mexico. Currently she is a visiting research fellow in the School of Geography at the University of Leeds and is part of the EU-funded network Contested Cities (Ciudades en Disputa: http://contested-cities.net). Since 2008 she has been the director of the "Galería," the photography gallery of Huellas Mexicanas (www.huellasmexicanas.org).

References

Introduction

Alexander, P. 2010. "Rebellion of the Poor: South Africa's Service Delivery Protests; A Preliminary Analysis." *Review of African Political Economy* 37 (123): 25–40, doi:10.1080/03056241003637870.

Davis, M. 2006. *Planet of Slums.* New York: Verso.

Elizalde, L., M. Fry, L. Musto, M. Saguinetti, G. Sarachu, and F. Texeira. 2012. "Clasificadores/as de residuos urbanos sólidos en Montevideo: condicionamientos, posibilidades y tentativas de organización." *Contrapunto* 1: 63–89.

Harvey, D. 2012. "Preface: Henry Lefebvre's Vision." In *Rebel Cities: From the Right to the City to the Urban Revolution,* edited by D. Harvey, ix–xviii. New York: Verso.

Chapter 1: Thembelihle Burning, Hope Rising

Alexander, P. 2010. "Rebellion of the Poor: South Africa's Service Delivery Protests; A Preliminary Analysis." *Review of African Political Economy* 37 (123): 25–40, doi:10.1080/03056241003637870.

Ballard, R., A. Habib, and I. Valodia. 2006. *Voices of Protest: Social Movements in Post-apartheid South Africa.* Scottsville, South Africa: University of KwaZulu-Natal Press.

Bond, P. 2000. *Cities of Gold, Townships of Coal: Essays on South Africa's New Urban Crisis.* Newark, NJ: Africa World Press.

Dawson, M. and L. Sinwell. 2012. *Contesting Transformation: Popular Resistance in Twenty-First-Century South Africa.* London: Pluto Press.

Gauteng Province. 2015. "Government to Accelerate Provision of Services in Thembelihle Following a Meeting." Official government statement and press release, April 24.

Le Roux, A. 2014. *Contesting Space: A Ward Committee and Social Movement*

Organisation in Thembelihle, Johannesburg. Unpublished M.A. dissertation, University of Johannesburg, Johannesburg, South Africa.

Murray, M. 2008. *Taming the Disorderly City: The Spatial Landscape of Johannesburg after Apartheid.* Ithaca, NY: Cornell University Press.

Pingo, N. 2013. *Institutionalisation of a Social Movement: The Case of Thembelihle, the Thembelihle Crisis Committee and the Operation Khanyisa Movement and the Use of the Brick, the Ballot and the Voice.* Unpublished M.A. dissertation, Witwatersrand University, Johannesburg, South Africa.

Saul, J. and P. Bond. 2014. *South Africa: The Present as History; From Mrs Ples to Mandela and Marikana.* Woodbridge, Suffolk, UK: James Currey.

Segodi, S. 2015. "The Siege of Thembelihle." *Amandla* 39: 12–13. Available at http://amandla.org.za.

Sinwell, L. 2011. "Is 'Another World' Really Possible? Re-examining Counter-hegemonic Forces in Post-apartheid South Africa." *Review of African Political Economy* 38 (127): 61–76.

Tomlinson, R., R. Beauregard, L. Bremmer, and X. Mangcu, eds. 2003. *Emerging Johannesburg: Perspectives on the Postapartheid City.* London: Routledge.

United Front Press Statement. 2015. "Press Statement: End the De Facto State of Emergency in Thembelihle." Available at http://unitedfrontsa.wordpress.com.

Chapter 2: Against All Odds

Adler, G., and J. Steinberg. 2000. *From Comrades to Citizens: The South African Civics Movement and the Transition to Democracy.* London: Macmillan.

Alexander, P. 2013. "Marikana, Turning Point in South African History." *Review of African Political Economy* 40 (138): 605–19.

———. 2014a. "Marikana Shows Gaps in Piketty Thesis." *Mail & Guardian*, July 25. http://mg.co.za/article/2014-07-24-marikana-shows-gaps-in-piketty-thesis.

———. 2014b. "Marikana Commission of Inquiry: From Narratives Towards History." Paper presented at the African Studies Association (United Kingdom) conference, University of Sussex, September 9–11.

Alexander, P., T. Lekgowa, B. Mmope, L. Sinwell, and B. Xezwi. 2012. *Marikana: A View from the Mountain and a Case to Answer.* Johannesburg: Jacana Media.

Allen, V. L. 2005. *The History of Black Mineworkers in South Africa.* 3 vols. London: Merlin Press.

Ashman, S. 2012. "Combined and Uneven Development." In *The Elgar Companion to Marxist Economics*, edited by B. Fine and A. Saad-Filho, 60–65. Cheltenham, UK: Edward Elgar.

Ashman, S., and N. Pons-Vignon. 2015. "NUMSA, the Working Class and Socialist Politics in South Africa." *Socialist Register* 51: 99–113.

Banaji, J. 2010. *Theory as History: Essays on Modes of Production and Exploitation.* Leiden: Brill.

Bank, L. 2011. *Home Spaces, Street Styles: Contesting Power and Identity in a South African City.* London: Pluto Press.

Barker, C. 1995. "'The Muck of Ages': Reflections on Proletarian Self-Emancipation." *Studies in Marxism* 2: 81–112.

———. 2008. "Some Thoughts on Marxism and Social Movements." Paper presented at the Micro-Conference on Marxism and Social Movements, Charlton Public Library, Manchester, UK, March 16.

Bench Marks (Bench Marks Foundation). 2012. *Communities in the Platinum Minefields.* Johannesburg: Bench Marks. http://www.bench-marks.org.za/research/rustenburg_review_policy_gap_final_aug_2012.pdf.

Bezuidenhout, A., and S. Buhlungu. 2008. "Union Solidarity under Stress: The Case of the National Union of Mineworkers in South Africa." *Labor Studies Journal* 33 (3): 262–87.

———. 2011. "From Compounded to Fragmented Labour: Mineworkers and the Demise of Compounds in South Africa." *Antipode* 43 (2): 237–63.

Bruce, D. 2001. *The Operation of the Criminal Justice System in Dealing with the Violence at Amplats.* Research report written for the Centre for the Study of Violence and Reconciliation, Johannesburg.

Bond, P. 2000. *Elite Transition: From Apartheid to Neoliberalism in South Africa.* London: Pluto Press.

Bowman, A., and G. Isaacs. 2014. "Demanding the Impossible? Platinum Mining Profits and Wage Demands in Context Research on Money and Finance." Research on Money and Finance Occasional Policy Paper No. 11, Wits University, Johannesburg, June 4.

Buhlungu, S. 2010. *A Paradox of Victory: COSATU and the Democratic Transformation in South Africa.* Scottsville, South Africa: University of KwaZulu-Natal Press.

Ceruti, C. 2011. "The Hidden Element in the 2010 Public-Sector Strike in South Africa." *Review of African Political Economy* 38 (127): 151–57.

Cohen, S. 2011. "The Red Mole: Workers' Councils as a Means of Revolutionary Transformation." In Ness and Azzellini 2011: 48–65.

Cox, K. R., D. Hemson, and A. Todes. 2004. "Urbanisation in South Africa and the Changing Character of Migrant Labour." *South African Geographical Journal* 86 (1): 7–16.

Crais, C. 2002. *The Politics of Evil: Magic State Power and the Political Imagination in South Africa*. Cambridge: Cambridge University Press.

Desai, R. 2014. *Miners Shot Down*, film documentary on the Marikana massacre. Johannesburg: Uhuru Productions. See www.minersshotdown.co.za.

Forrest, K. 2014. "Rustenburg's Fractured Recruitment Regime: Who Benefits?" *African Studies* 73 (2): 149–68.

Kibet, M. 2013. "Migration into Rustenburg Local Municipality between 1996 and 2001." *Journal of Social Development in Africa* 28 (1): 65–85.

Legassick, M. 2007. *Towards Socialist Democracy*. Scottsville, South Africa: University of KwaZulu-Natal Press.

Marx, K. 1844. Introduction to *A Contribution to the Critique of Hegel's Philosophy of Right*. Available through the Marxists Internet Archive at www.marxists.org.

Mayekiso, M. 1996. *Township Politics: Civic Struggles for a New South Africa*. New York: Monthly Review Press.

Mbenga, B., and A. Manson. 2010. *"People of the Dew": A History of the Bafokeng of Phokeng-Rustenburg Region, South Africa, from Early Times to 2000*. Johannesburg: Jacana Media.

Moodie, D., and V. Ndatshe. 1994. *Going for Gold: Men, Mines, and Migration*. Johannesburg: Ravan Press.

Mosiane, B. 2011. "Livelihoods and the Transformative Potential of Cities: Challenges of Inclusive Development in Rustenburg, North West Province, South Africa." *Singapore Journal of Tropical Geography* 32: 38–52.

Ness, I., and D. Azzellini. 2011. *Ours to Master and to Own: Workers' Control from the Commune to the Present*. Chicago: Haymarket Books.

Ngwane, T. 2012. "Labour Strikes and Community Protests: Is There a Basis for Unity in Post-Apartheid South Africa?" In *Contesting Transformation: Popular Resistance in Twenty-First Century South Africa*, edited by M. C. Dawson and L. Sinwell, 125–42. London: Pluto Press.

Pelser, E., J. Schnetler, and A. Louw. 2002. *Not Everybody's Business: Community Policing in the SAPS' Priority Areas*. Monograph 71. Pretoria: Institute for Security Studies.

Phalatse, S. 2000. "From Industrialisation to De-industrialisation in the Former South African Homelands: The Case of Mogwase, North West." *Urban Forum* 11 (1): 149–61.

Piketty, T. 2014. *Capital in the Twenty-First Century*. Cambridge, MA: Belknap Press.

Rakodi, C. 1995. "Poverty Lines or Household Strategies? A Review of Conceptual Issues in the Study of Urban Poverty." *Habitat International* 19 (4): 407–26.

Republic of South Africa. 2005. Notice 965: Guidelines for the Establishment and Operation of Municipal Ward Committees. Available at www.gov.za.

Runciman, C., T. Ngwane, and P. Alexander. 2012. "A Protest Event Analysis of South Africa's Rebellion of the Poor: Some Initial Results." Paper presented at the South African Sociological Conference, University of Cape Town, July 3.

Rustenburg Local Municipality. 2011. Housing Sector Plan for the Rustenburg Local Municipality (Draft). Rustenburg: UWP Consultants, November.

SAPA (South African Press Association). 2013. "Marikana Women Want Bright Future." August 13. Available at www.iol.co.za/news/south-africa/north-west/marikana-women-want-bright-future-1561777. [*Editor's note: The South African Press Association ceased operations on March 30, 2015, after seventy-seven years in existence.*]

Shivambu, F., and J. Smith. 2014. *The Coming Revolution: Julius Malema and the Fight for Economic Freedom.* Johannesburg: Jacana Media.

Sinwell, L. 2015. "'AMCU by Day, Workers' Committee by Night': Insurgent Trade Unionism at Anglo Platinum (Amplats) Mine, 2012–2014." *Review of African Political Economy* 42 (146): 591–605.

Sinwell, L., and S. Mbatha. 2016. *The Spirit of Marikana: The Rise of Insurgent Trade Unionism in South Africa.* Johannesburg: Wits University Press.

Skocpol, T. 1979. *States and Social Revolutions.* Cambridge: Cambridge University Press.

Statistics South Africa. 2011. Rustenburg Municipality Census. Available at www.statssa.gov.za.

Tabane, R. 2013. "Amcu a Group of Vigilantes and Liars, Say Alliance Bosses." *Mail & Guardian*, May 1.

Terreblanche, S. 2012. *Lost in Transformation: South Africa's Search for a New Future since 1986.* Johannesburg: KMM Review Publishing Company.

Wolpe, H. 1972. "Capitalism and Cheap Labour-Power in South Africa: From Segregation to Apartheid." *Economy and Society* 1 (4): 425–56.

Chapter 3: Makoko Slum Settlement

Adelekan, I. 2010. "Vulnerability of Poor Urban Coastal Communities to Flooding in Lagos, Nigeria." *Environment and Urbanization* 22 (2): 433–50.

Adepoju, A. 2002. "Fostering Free Movement of Persons in West Africa: Achievements, Constraints, and Prospects for Intraregional Migration." *International Migration* 40 (2): 3–28.

Agbola, T. and E. Agunbiade. (2007) 2009. "Urbanization, Slum Development, and Security of Tenure: The Challenges of Meeting Millennium Development Goal 7 in Metropolitan Lagos, Nigeria." In *Urban Population-Environment Dynamics in the Developing World: Case Studies and Lessons Learned*, edited by A. De Sherbiniin et al., 78–108. Paris: Committee for International Cooperation in National Research in Demography (CICRED).

Aina, T. A. 1989. "'Many Routes Enter the Market Place': Housing Submarkets for the Urban Poor in Metropolitan Lagos, Nigeria." *Environment and Urbanization* 1 (2): 38–49, doi: 10.1177/095624788900100205.

Akanni, C. O. 2010. "Spatial and Seasonal Analysis of Traffic-Related Pollutant Concentrations in Lagos Metropolis, Nigeria." *African Journal of Agricultural Research* 5 (11): 1264–72.

Annen, K. 2001. "Inclusive and Exclusive Social Capital in the Small-Firm Sector in Developing Countries." *Journal of Institutional and Theoretical Economics (JITE) / Zeitschrift für die gesamte Staatswissenschaft* 157 (2): 319–30.

Aßheuer, T., I. Thiele-Eich, and B. Braun. 2013. "Coping with the Impacts of Severe Flood Events in Dhaka's Slums: The Role of Social Capital." *Erdkunde* 67 (1): 21–35.

Atubi, A. O. 2010. "Road Transport System Management and Traffic in Lagos, South Western Nigeria." *African Research Review* 4 (4): 459–70.

Awofeso, P. 2011. "One out of Every Two Nigerians Now Lives in a City: There Are Many Problems but Just One Solution." *World Policy Journal* 27 (4): 67–73.

Ayeni, A. O. 2014. "Domestic Water Source, Sanitation, and High Risk of Bacteriological Diseases in the Urban Slum: Case of Cholera in Makoko, Lagos, Nigeria." *Journal of Environment Pollution and Human Health* 2 (1): 12–15.

Babalobi, B. 2013. "Water, Sanitation, and Hygiene Practices among Primary-School Children in Lagos: A Case Study of the Makoko Slum Community." *Water International* 38 (7): 921–29.

BBC. 2012. "Lagos Makoko Slums Knocked Down in Nigeria." July 17. Available at www.bbc.com/news.

Blier, S. P. 1985. "Kings, Crowns, and Rights of Succession: Obalufon Arts at Ife and Other Yoruba Centers." *Art Bulletin* 67 (3): 383–401.

Breslin, M. and R. Buchanan. 2008. "On the Case Study Method of Research and Teaching in Design." *Design Issues* 24 (1): 36–40.

Buttenheim, A. M. 2008. "The Sanitation Environment in Urban Slums: Implications for Child Health." *Population and Environment* 30 (1–2): 26–47.

Castles, S. 2009. "Development and Migration—Migration and Development: What Comes First? Global Perspective and African Experiences." *Theoria: A Journal of Social and Political Theory* 56 (121): 1–31.

Chatterji, R. 2005. "Voice, Event, and Narrative: Towards an Understanding of Everyday Life in Dharavi." *Sociological Bulletin* 54 (3): 428–35.

Chojnacka, H. 2000. "Early Marriage and Polygyny: Feature Characteristics of Nuptiality in Africa." *Genus* 56 (3–4): 179–208.

Collins, J. 2015. "Makoko Floating School, Beacon of Hope for the Lagos 'Water-world': A History of Cities in 50 Buildings, Day 48." *Guardian*, June 2.

Culhane, D. P. 1992. "The Quandaries of Shelter Reform: An Appraisal of Efforts to 'Manage' Homelessness." *Social Service Review* 66 (3): 428–40.

Douglas, I., K. Alam, M. Maghenda, Y. McDonnell, L. McLean, and J. Campbell. 2008. "Unjust Waters: Climate Change, Flooding, and the Urban Poor in Africa." *Environment and Urbanization* 20 (1): 187–205.

Gandy, M. 2006. "Planning, Anti-planning, and the Infrastructure Crisis Facing Metropolitan Lagos." *Urban Studies* 43 (2): 371–96.

Grazian, D. 2009. "Urban Nightlife, Social Capital, and the Public Life of Cities." *Sociological Forum* 24 (4): 908–17.

Gunther, I. 2012. "Deadly Cities? Spatial Inequalities in Mortality in Sub-Saharan Africa." *Population and Development Bureau* 38 (3): 469–86.

Hahn, H. P. 2010. "Urban Life-Worlds in Motion: In Africa and Beyond." *Africa Spectrum* 45 (3): 115–29.

Hall, D. 2000. "Cross-Border Movement and the Dynamics of Transition Processes in Southeastern Europe." *GeoJournal* 50 (2–3): 249–53.

Hayes, B. C. 2000. "Religious Independents within Western Industrialized Nations: A Socio-Demographic Profile." *Sociology of Religion* 61 (2): 191–207.

Hollifield, J. F. 2004. "The Emerging Migration State." *International Migration Review* 38 (3): 885–912.

Ibiwoye, D. 2014. "Makoko: A Slum That Refuses to Dissolve." *Vanguard*, May 20. Available at www.vanguardngr.com.

Jarrett, R. L. and S. M. Jefferson. 2004. "Women's Danger Management Strategies in an Inner-City Housing Project." *Family Relations* 53 (2): 138–47.

Kandiyoti, D. 1988. "Bargaining with Patriarchy." *Gender and Society* 2 (3): 274–90.

Kumar, N. and A. S. Sidhu. 2005. "Pull and Push Factors in Labour Migration: A Study of Brick-Kiln Workers in Punjab." *Indian Journal of Industrial Relations* 41 (2): 221–32.

Marx, B., T. Stoker, and T. Suri. 2012. "The Economics of Slums in the Developing World." *Journal of Economic Perspectives* 27 (4): 187–210.

Meschkank, J. 2011. "Investigations into Slum Tourism in Mumbai: Poverty Tourism and Tensions between Different Constructions of Reality." *GeoJournal* 76 (1): 47–62.

Nijman, J. 2015. "India's Urban Future: Views from the Slum." *American Behavioral Scientist* 59 (3): 406–23.

Nubi, T. G., and C. Ajoku. 2011. "Nexus between Effective Land Management and Housing Delivery in Lagos." *Environment and Urbanization* 23 (1): 285–303.

Nwizu, E. N., Z. Iliyasu, S. A. Ibrahim, and H. S. Galadanci. 2011. "Socio-Demographic and Maternal Factors in Anaemia in Pregnancy at Booking in Kano, Northern Nigeria." *African Journal of Reproductive Health / La Revue Africaine de la Santé Reproductive* 15 (4): 33–41.

Ocheje, P. D. 2007. "'In the Public Interest': Forced Evictions, Land Rights, and Human Development in Africa." *Journal of African Law* 51 (2): 173–214.

Oduwaye, L. 2007. "Effects of Institutional Land Uses on Road Traffic in Metropolitan Lagos." *Social Sciences* 2 (3): 255–63.

Okoli, R. 2013. "Makoko: A Model for a Culturally Sensitive Urban Renewal in Lagos." *Spaces & Flows: An International Journal of Urban and Extra Urban Studies* 3 (1): 135–50.

Okulaja, A. 2013. "Human Rights Commission Inspects Demolished Slums in Lagos." *Premium Times*, November 23. Available at www.premiumtimesng.com.

Otoo-Oyortey, N., and S. Pobi. 2003. "Early Marriage and Poverty: Exploring Links and Key Policy Issues." *Gender and Development* 11 (2): 42–51.

Parnell, S. 2003. "Race, Power, and Urban Control: Johannesburg's Inner City Slum-Yards, 1910–1923." *Journal of Southern African Studies* 29 (3): 615–37.

Pokhariyal, G. P. 2005. "Models for Understanding Social Problems in Slums." *International Journal on World Peace* 22 (2): 59–75.

Pothukuchi, K. 2003. "Working Women's Hostels in Bangalore, India: Incorporating Life-Cycle Issues in Shelter Policy." *Journal of Architectural and Planning Research* 20 (2): 91–109.

Punch, K. F. 2005. *Introduction to Social Research: Quantitative and Qualitative Approaches*. London: Sage Publications.

Reckner, P. 2002. "Remembering Gotham: Urban Legends, Public History, and Representations of Poverty, Crime, and Race in New York City." *International Journal of Historical Archaeology* 6 (2): 95–112.

Sen, A. 2012. "'Exist, Endure, Erase the City' (*Sheher mein jiye, is ko sahe, ya ise mitaye?*): Child Vigilantes and Micro-Cultures of Urban Violence in a Riot-Affected Hyderabad Slum." *Ethnography* 13 (1): 71–86.

Shaban, A. 2008. "Ghettoisation, Crime, and Punishment in Mumbai." *Economic and Political Weekly* 43 (33): 68–73.

Silvey, R. 2006. "Geographies of Gender and Migration: Spatializing Social Difference." *International Migration Review* 40 (1): 64–81.

Tripathi, S. 2014. "Praise the Lord and Buy Insurance." *Index on Censorship* 34 (4): 188–92.

Udo-Udoma, O. *World Bank Public Participation Policies and Processes in Relation to the Lives of Beneficiaries in Slum Upgrading Projects. Case Study: Makoko, Lagos, Nigeria.* Unpublished M.Phil. thesis, Department of Civil Engineering, University of Cape Town, South Africa.

Vanguard. 2012. "Demolition Starts at Makoko Slum." July 16. Available at www.vanguardngr.com.

Verma, M. K. 2012. Review of *Living with Violence: An Anthropology of Events and Everyday Life*, by Roma Chatterji and Deepak Mehta. *International Sociology* 27 (5): 635–37.

Walker, J. 2012. "Early Marriage in Africa—Trends, Harmful Effects, and Interventions." *African Journal of Reproductive Health / La Revue Africaine de la Santé Reproductive* 16 (2): 231–40.

Weeks, J. R., A. Hill, D. Stow, A. Getis, and D. Fugate. 2007. "Can We Spot a Neighborhood from the Air? Defining Neighborhood Structure in Accra, Ghana." *GeoJournal* 69 (1–2): 9–22.

Werlin, H. 2006. "The Slums of Nairobi: Explaining Urban Misery." *World Affairs* 169 (1): 29–48.

Zulu, E. M., F. N. Dodoo, and A. Chika-Ezer. 2002. "Sexual Risk-Taking in the Slums of Nairobi, Kenya, 1993–98." *Population Studies* 56 (3): 311–23.

Chapter 4: The Ayotzinapa Massacre

Anderson, B. 1983. *Imagined Communities.* New York: Verso.

Bartra, Armando. 1996. *Guerrero bronco: Campesinos, ciudadanos y guerrilleros en la Costa Grande.* Mexico: Ediciones Era.

———. 2000. *Crónicas del sur: Utopías campesinas en Guerrero.* Mexico: Ediciones Era.

Díaz, Gloria. 2015. "El basurero, una incógnita." *Proceso.* Año 38. Edición Especial 48. Mexico.

Fuentes Vivar, R. 2015. "Peña Nieto, 11 reformas y 22 pendientes." *Mundo ejecutivo*, January 12. Available at http://mundoejecutivo.com.mx.

Gilly, A. 1997. *Chiapas: La razón ardiente; ensayo sobre la rebelión en el mundo encantado.* Mexico: Ediciones Era.

González Rodríguez, S. 2015. *Los 43 de Iguala: México; verdad y reto de los estudiantes desaparecidos.* Crónicas. Barcelona: Anagrama.

Hernández Corchado, R. 2014. *'My People Is a People on Its Knees': Mexican Labor*

Migration from the Montaña Region and the Formation of a Working Class in New York City. Doctoral dissertation, City University of New York.

Illades, C. 2012. *La inteligencia rebelde: La izquierda en el debate público en México, 1968–1989*. Mexico: Océano.

Imprenta de Luz. 2014. *Ayotzinapa—Ciudad de México*. Video documentary. Available at www.youtube.com/watch?v=7fEx2ytp9DU.

Montemayor, C. 1991. *Guerra en el paraíso*. Mexico: Seix Barral.

———. 2010. *La violencia de estado en México: Antes y después de 1968*. Mexico: Random House Mondadori.

Nimmo, J. 2016. "Tribute to the Ayotzinapa 43+3+2+1000's More." Available at www.jannimmo.com/Ayotzinapa.html.

Pacheco, J. E. (1972) 1997. "Tenga para que se entretenga." In *El principio del placer*. Mexico City: Ediciones Era.

Robinson, W. I. 2014. "In the Wake of Ayotzinapa, ¿Adónde va México?" *El BeiSMan*. Available at www.elbeisman.com/article.php?action=read&id=477.

Ross, J. 1995. *Shadows of Tender Fury: The Letters and Communiqués of Subcomandante Marcos and the Zapatista Army of National Liberation*. New York: Monthly Review Press.

Sierra, M. T. 2015. "Emergentes respuestas locales a la violencia y la impunidad: Ayotzinapa y la crisis de la seguridad pública en Guerrero, México." *Latin American Studies Association Forum* 46 (2): 19–23. Available at http://lasa .international.pitt.edu.

Tlachinollan Centro de Derechos Humanos de la Montaña. 2015. "XXI Informe: Desde las trincheras de Ayotzinapa; la defensa por la educación y la vida de los hijos del pueblo." Available at www.tlachinollan.org.

Chapter 5: The Case of the West Zone

Alonso, A. and A. Mische. 2015. "June Demonstrations in Brazil: Repertoires of Contention and Government's Response to Protest." Paper presented at "From Contention to Social Change: Rethinking the Consequences of Social Movements and Cycles of Protests," Midterm Conference of the ESA Research Network on Social Movements, held February 19–20 at the Universidad Complutense de Madrid, Spain.

Arias, E. D. 2004. "Faith in Our Neighbors: Networks and Social Order in Three Brazilian Favelas." *Latin American Politics & Society* 46 (1): 1–38.

———. 2006. "The Dynamics of Criminal Governance: Networks and Social Order in Rio De Janeiro." *Journal of Latin American Studies* 38 (2): 293–325.

Cano, I. and T. Duarte. 2012. *No sapatinho: A evolução das milícias no Rio de Janeiro (2008–2011)*. Policy paper. Rio de Janeiro: Heinrich Böll Stiftung.

Della Porta, D. and S. Tarrow. 2005. "Transitional Processes and Social Activism: An Introduction." In *Transitional Protest and Global Activism*, edited by Donatella della Porta and Sidney Tarrow, 1–21. Lanham, MD: Rowman and Littlefield.

Gomes, S. S. R. 2015. "Apuntes sobre la militancia de los jóvenes en contextos de violencia: El caso de Rio de Janeiro, Brasil y de Guerrero, México. In *Actores, redes y desafíos: Juventudes y infancias en América Latina*, edited by A. Hernández and A. Campos. Tijuana: El Colegio de la Frontera Norte.

Joseph, G. M. 1990. "On the Trail of Latin American Bandits: A Reexamination of Peasant Resistance." *Latin American Research Review* 25 (3): 7–53.

Loveman, M. 1998. "High-Risk Collective Action: Defending Human Rights in Chile, Uruguay, and Argentina." *American Journal of Sociology* 104 (2): 477–525.

Leeds, E. 1996. "Cocaine and Parallel Polities in the Brazilian Urban Periphery: Constraints on Local-Level Democratization." *Latin American Research Review* 31(3): 47–83.

Pinheiro, P. S. 1997. "Popular Responses to State-Sponsored Violence in Brazil." In *The New Politics of Inequality in Latin America: Rethinking Participation and Representation*, edited by D. A. Chalmers et al., 261–80. Oxford: Oxford University Press.

Sewell, W. H. 2001. "Space in Contentious Politics." In *Silence and Voice in the Study of Contentious Politics*, edited by R. Aminzade, 51–88. Cambridge: Cambridge University Press.

Scott, J. C. 1985. *Weapons of the Weak: Everyday Forms of Peasant Resistance*. New Haven, CT: Yale University Press.

———. 1986. *Resistance without Protest: Peasant Opposition to the Zakat in Malaysia and to the Tithe in France*. Townsville, Queensland: Asian Studies Association of Australia.

Tarrow, S. G. 2005. *The New Transnational Activism*. Cambridge: Cambridge University Press.

Tilly, C. 2004. *Contention and Democracy in Europe, 1650–2000*. Cambridge: Cambridge University Press.

Zaluar, A. 1985. *Máquina e a revolta: As organizações populares e o significado da pobreza*. São Paulo, Brazil: Brasiliense.

Chapter 6: The Uruguayan Recyclers' Union

Anderson, B. 1983. *Imagined Communities*. London: Verso.

Appadurai, A. 1986. "Introduction: Commodities and the Politics of Value." In *The Social Life of Things: Commodities in Cultural Perspective*, edited by A. Appadurai, 3–63. Cambridge: Cambridge University Press.

Atzeni, M., ed. 2014. *Workers and Labour in a Globalized Capitalism*. London: Palgrave.

Carsten, J., ed. 2013. "Blood Will Out: Essays on Liquid Transfers and Flows." Special issue, *Journal of the Royal Anthropological Institute* 19.

Castells, M. 2000. *The Rise of the Network Society*. Oxford: Blackwell.

Collins, T. W. 1988. "An Analysis of the Memphis Garbage Strike of 1968." In *Anthropology for the Nineties*, ed. J. B. Cole, 360–80. New York: Free Press.

Darlington, R. 2014. "The Role of Trade Unions in Building Resistance: Theoretical, Historical, and Comparative Perspectives." In *Workers and Labour in a Globalized Capitalism*, 111–38.

Deleuze, G., and C. Parnet. 1987. *Dialogues*. London: Athlone Press.

Elizalde, L., M. Fry, L. Musto, M. Saguinetti, G. Sarachu, and F. Texeira. 2012. "Clasificadores/as de residuos urbanos sólidos en Montevideo: Condicionamientos, posibilidades y tentativas de organización." *Contrapunto* 1: 63–89.

Epstein, D. 2003. "The Piquetero Movement of Greater Buenos Aires: Working Class Protest during the Current Argentine Crisis." *Canadian Journal of Latin American and Caribbean Studies* 28 (55–56): 11–36.

———. 2009. "Perpetuating Social Movements amid Declining Opportunity: The Survival Strategies of Two Argentine Piquetero Groups." *Revista Europea de Estudios Latinoamericanos y del Caribe / European Review of Latin American and Caribbean Studies* 86: 3–19.

Errandonea, A., and D. Costabile. 1968. *Sindicato y sociedad en el Uruguay*. Montevideo: Biblioteca de Cultura Universitaria.

Fernández, L. 2007. "De hurgadores a clasificadores organizados: Análisis político institucional del trabajo con la basura en Montevideo." In *Recicloscopio: Miradas sobre recuperadores urbanos de residuos de América Latina*, edited by P. J. Schamber and F. M. Suárez, 83–98. Buenos Aires: Promoteo.

Gall, G., ed. 2002. *Union Organizing: Campaigning for Trade Union Recognition*. London: Routledge.

Gallin, D. 2001. "Propositions on Trade Unions and Informal Employment in Times of Globalisation." *Antipode* 33: 531–49.

Gille, Z. 2010. "Actor Networks, Modes of Production, and Waste Regimes: Reassembling the Macro-Social." *Environment and Planning A* 42 (5): 1049–64.

González Sierra, Y. 1989. *Reseña histórica del movimiento sindical uruguayo (1870–1984)*. Montevideo: CIEDUR.

Hansen, K., W. E. Little, and L. B. Milgram, eds. 2014. *Street Economies in the Urban Global South*. Santa Fe, NM: SAR Press.

Hart, K. 1973. "Informal Income Opportunities and Urban Employment in Ghana." *Journal of Modern African Studies* 11 (1): 61–89.

Harvey, D. 2008. "The Right to the City." *New Left Review* 53 (September–October): 23–40.

———. 2012. *Rebel Cities: From the Right to the City to the Urban Revolution*. London: Verso.

Heynen, N., M. Kaika, and E. Swyngedouw. 2006. *In the Nature of Cities: Urban Political Ecology and the Politics of Urban Metabolism*. New York: Routledge.

Kelly, J., and E. Heery. 1989. "Full-Time Officers and Trade Union Recruitment." *British Journal of Industrial Relations* 27 (2): 196–213.

Kopytoff, I. 1986. "The Cultural Biography of Things: Commoditization as Process." In *The Social Life of Things: Commodities in Cultural Perspective*, edited by A. Appadurai, 64–94. Cambridge: Cambridge University Press.

Lazar, S. 2008. *El Alto, Rebel City: Self and Citizenship in Andean Bolivia*. Durham, NC: Duke University Press.

Lee, B., and E. LiPuma. 2002. "Cultures of Circulation: The Imaginations of Modernity." *Public Culture* 14 (1): 191–213.

Lefebvre, H. 1968. *Le droit à la ville*. Paris: Seuil.

Levi-Strauss, C. 1969. *The Elementary Structures of Kinship*. Boston: Beacon Press.

Malinowski, B. 1922. *Argonauts of the Western Pacific*. London: Routledge.

Martin López, T. 2014. *The Winter of Discontent: Myth, Memory, and History*. Liverpool, UK: Liverpool University Press.

Mason, B., and P. Bain. 1991. "Trade Union Recruitment Strategies: Facing the 1990s." *Industrial Relations Journal* 22 (1): 36–45.

Medina, M. 2000. "Scavenger Cooperatives in Asia and Latin America." *Resources, Conservation, and Recycling* 31 (1): 51–69.

Newman, P. W. G. 1999. "Sustainability and Cities: Extending the Metabolism Model." *Landscape and Urban Planning* 44 (4): 219–26.

Ras, N. 1996. *El gaucho y la ley*. Montevideo: Carlos Marchesi.

Silverman, J. 2011. "Labor Relations in Uruguay under the Frente Amplio Government, 2005–2009: From Neoliberalism to Neocorporativism?" Paper delivered at the VII Global Labour University Conference, University of the Witwatersrand, Johannesburg, South Africa.

Svampa, M., and P. Sebastián. 2003. *Entre la ruta y el barrio: La experiencia de las organizaciones piqueteras*. Buenos Aires: Biblos.

————. 2004. "La experiencia piquetera: el desafío de las organizaciones de desocupados en Argentina." *Revista da Sociedade Brasileira de Economia Política* 15: 88–110.

Wolman, A. 1965. "The Metabolism of Cities." *Scientific American* 213 (3): 179–90.

Chapter 7: The Nonadanga Eviction in Kolkata

Action Aid. 2008. "Rich Tribal Poor: Displacing People, Destroying Identity in India's Indigenous Heartland." Action Aid Report. New Delhi: Action Aid India.

Banerjee, S. 2012. "Revolutionary Movements in a Post-Marxian Era." *Economic and Political Weekly* 47 (18): 55–61.

Banerjee-Guha, S. 2008. "Space Relations of Capital and Significance of New Economic Enclaves: SEZs in India." *Economic and Political Weekly* 43 (47): 51–60.

————, ed. 2009a. *Accumulation by Dispossession: Transformative Cities in the New Global Order*. New Delhi: Sage Publishing.

————. 2009b. "Contradictions in Enclave Development in Contemporary Times." *Human Geography* 2 (4): 1–16.

————. 2009c. "Neoliberalising the Urban: New Geographies of Power and Injustice in Indian Cities." *Economic and Political Weekly* 44 (22): 95–107.

————. 2009d. "Transformative Cities in the New Global Order." In *Accumulation by Dispossession*, 1–16.

————. 2013a. "Accumulation and Dispossession: Contradictions of Growth and Development in Contemporary India." *Journal of South Asian Studies* 36 (2): 165–79.

————. 2013b. "Unnoyon, Sthanikota, Punjir Somosamoyik Punjibhaban O Be-Ektiyar Shromojeebi Manush [Development, Spatiality, Contemporary Accumulation of Capital, and the Marginalized Working Class]." *Porichoy* 81 (4–6): 185–203.

————. Forthcoming. "Remaking the 'Urban' in 21st Century India." In Rajiv Thakur et. al., Urban and Regional Development: 20th Century Forms and 21st Century Transformations.

Burte, H. 2014. "The Smart City Card." *Economic and Political Weekly* 49 (46): 22–26.

Benjamin, S. 2006. "Manufacturing Neoliberalism: Lifestyling Indian Urbanity." In *Accumulation by Dispossession*, 92–124.

CASUMM. *JNNURM: A Blueprint for Unconstitutional, Undemocratic Governance*. Report of the Collaborative for the Advancement of the Study of

Urbanism through Mixed Media, Bangalore.

Chatterton, P. 2002. "Squatting Is Still Legal, Necessary, and Free: A Brief Intervention in the Corporate City." *Antipode* 34 (1): 1–7.

Fainstein, S. 2003. "Can We Make the Cities We Want?" In *The Urban Moment: Cosmopolitan Essays on the Late-20th-Century City*, edited by R. A. Beauregard and S. Body-Gendrot, 273–86. Thousand Oaks, CA: Sage Publications.

Gillan, M., and R. Lambert. 2013. "Labour Movements and the Age of Crisis: Scale, Form, and Repertoires of Action in India and Beyond." *Journal of South Asian Studies* 36 (2): 180–98.

Government of India. 2008. "Minutes of the 20th meeting of the SEZ Board of Approval held on 2nd January, 2008, at 10:30 a.m., to consider proposals for setting up of Special Economic Zones." Available at www.sezindia.nic.in.

Harvey, D. 1985. *The Urbanisation of Capital*. London: Basil Blackwell.

———. 2005. *A Brief History of Neoliberalism*. Oxford: Oxford University Press.

———. 2010. "Right to the City: From Capital Surplus to Accumulation by Dispossession," in *Accumulation by Dispossession*, 17–32.

———. 2012. *Rebel Cities: From the Right to the City to the Urban Revolution*. London: Verso.

Hollands, R. G. 2008. "Will the Real Smart City Please Stand Up?" *City* 12 (3): 302–20.

Patnaik, U. 2008. "Imperialism, Resources, and Food Security with Reference to the Indian Experience." *Human Geography* 1 (1): 40–53.

Sanyal, K. 2007. *Rethinking Capitalist Development: Primitive Accumulation, Governmentality, and Post-colonial Capitalism*. New Delhi: Routledge.

Sassen, S. 1999. "Whose City Is It? Globalization and the Formation of New Claims." In *The Urban Moment: Cosmopolitan Essays on the Late-20th-Century City*, 99–118.

Singh, P. 2008. "City Development Plan and Urban Poor in Bhopal." Paper presented at the international workshop "Urban Neoliberalism: Restructuring South Asian Cities," held at the Tata Institute of Social Sciences, Mumbai, November 27–28.

Smith, N. 1996. *The New Urban Frontier: Gentrification and the Revanchist City*. London: Routledge.

———. 2002. "New Globalism, New Urbanism: Gentrification as Global Urban Strategy." *Antipode* 34 (3): 427–50.

Vagholikar, N. and P. J. Das. 2010. "Damming Northeast India: Juggernaut of Hydropower Projects Threaten Social and Environmental Security of Region." In Climate Himalaya website, December 20. Available at http://chimalaya.org.

Chapter 8: The Struggle of the Urban Poor against Forced Eviction in Jakarta

Ahniar, N. F., and R. J. Akbar. 2012. "BPS: Makin banyak pekerja di sector formal." *Viva*, May 7. Available at http://us.bisnis.news.viva.co.id/news/read/311346-bps--makin-banyak-pekerja-sektor-formal.

Ananta, D. D. 2015. "Penggusuran dan Mesin Pertumbuhan Kota." *IndoProgress*, September 4. Available at http://indoprogress.com.

Asia Monitor Resource Centre. 2012. Editorial: "Against Extractive Industries." *Asian Labour Update* 80: 1–3. Available at www.amrc.org.hk.

Bank Indonesia. 2015. "Laporan Perkembangan Properti Komersial Triwulan II." Available at www.bi.go.id/id/publikasi/survei/properti-komersial/Documents/Laporan_PPKom_Q2_2015.pdf.

Bayat, A. 1997. *Street Politics: Poor People's Movements in Iran*. New York: Columbia University Press.

Brenner, N., and N. Theodore. 2002. "Cities and the Geography of Actually Existing Neoliberalism." *Antipode* 34 (3): 349–79.

Davis, M. 2004. "Planet of Slums." *New Left Review* 26: 5–34.

———. 2006. *Planet of Slums*. London: Verso.

Haddad, L. 2012. "Poverty Is Urbanising and Needs Different Thinking on Development." *Guardian*, October 5.

Harding, A. 1995.

In *Theories of Urban Politics*, edited by D. Judge, G. Stoker, and H. Wolman, 35–53. London: Sage Publications.

Harvey, D. 1996. *Justice, Nature, and the Geography of Difference*. Oxford: Blackwell.

———. 2003. *The New Imperialism*. Oxford: Oxford University Press.

———. 2012. *Rebel Cities: From the Right to the City to the Urban Revolution*. London: Verso.

Jessop, B. 1990. *State Theory: Putting the Capitalist State in Its Place*. Cambridge: Polity Press.

Karina, S. 2012. "Ekspor Enam Komoditi Industri US$ 77,9 M." Available at http://bola.okezone.com/read/2012/01/03/452/551177/ekspor-enam-komoditi-industri-usd77-9-m.

Legal Aid Institute of Jakarta. "Kami yang Terusir: Laporan Penggusuran Paksa di Wilayah DKI Jakarta Januari-Agustus 2015." Annual report. Available at www.bantuanhukum.or.id/web/wp-content/uploads/2015/08/Laporan-Penggusuran-Paksa-Jakarta.pdf.

Logan, J., and H. Molotch. 1987. *Urban Fortunes: The Political Economy of Place*. Berkeley: University of California Press.

Miller, B., and W. Nicholls. 2013. "Social Movements in Urban Society: The City as a Space of Politicization." *Urban Geography* 34 (4): 452–73.

Mousseau, M. 2011. "Urban Poverty and Support for Islamist Terror." *Journal of Peace Research* 48 (1): 35–47.

Poulantzas, N. 1980. *State, Power, Socialism.* London: Verso.

Puspaningtyas, L. 2014. "Jakarta jadi kota dengan perkembangan investasi properti tertinggi." *Republika*, November 11. Available at www.republika.co.id.

Wilson, I. 2015. "The Politics of Flood Alleviation in Jakarta." *Jakarta Post*, September 5. Available at www.thejakartapost.com.

Notes

Chapter 2: Against All Odds

1   This essay is adapted from a paper delivered at the Twentieth International Conference on Alternative Futures and Popular Protest, held at Manchester Metropolitan University from March 30 to April 1, 2015, and hosted by Colin Barker.

2   This interpretation, as well as the programmatic thrust of the whole paper, were shaped by internal documents of the Socialist Group, most of them authored by Jonathan Grossman. The Socialist Group is a small collective of anti-Stalinist Marxists affiliated to the Democratic Left Front and the United Front; I am a member. Grossman can be reached at jonathan.grossman@uct.ac.za. I can be reached at trevorngwane@gmail.com.

3   The first phrase was used by Ronnie Kasrils, former ANC minister, when denouncing the killings in an interview for Rehad Desai's film *Miners Shot Down* (2014). The second phrase was used by Dali Mpofu, legal representative for the families of the dead miners, in arguments presented to the Marikana Commission; see www.marikanacomm.org.za.

4   Jobs dropped from 72,255 to 36,402 in mining (50%) and from 8,172 to 2,773 in the metal products and machinery sectors (66%). Sources: Mosiane 2011, 42; Phalatse 2000.

5   According to Forrest (2014, 153): "About 15 years ago 60 per cent of South African mine labour consisted of rural foreign nationals whilst 40 per cent was South African. Today about 30 per cent of mine labour is foreign and of the 70 per cent South African labour half is rural and half urban."

6   It has been estimated that as many as one in three mineworkers was subcontracted. The platinum sector had the higher number of such workers, at 36%, while gold had 15% (Bezuidenhout and Buhlungu 2008).

7   Independent researchers paint a bleaker picture, estimating that the housing backlog is 58,500 units and that the proportion of people living in shacks could be as high as 41% (Bench Marks 2012, 35).

8   The Royal Bafokeng Administration is a tribal council that has benefited from successful land claims that cover some platinum mines. The wealth and power emanating from this and the state recognition of "traditional authorities" makes the Bafokeng an important player in the platinum mining belt. See Mbenga and Manson 2010.

9   It is often referred to as Nkaneng-Bleskop to distinguish it from the informal settlement situated next to where the massacre occurred, Nkaneng-Wonderkop. Many informal settlements in South Africa use the name "Nkaneng," no doubt in reference to the "forceful" spirit and politics behind the establishment of these communities.

10   However, it should be noted that the definition of "migrant" covers a "huge variety" of "time-space geographies" that do not necessarily correspond with attitudes toward migrancy or people's sense of the distinction between rural and urban (Cox, Hemson, and Todes 2004, 7).

11   Cox, Hemson, and Todes (2004) provide a list of "deep rural areas" that they define in terms of poverty, geography, and rural status. Some areas mentioned in the Eastern Cape are Libode, Ngqeleni, Qumbu, Mqanduli, and Lusikisiki. It is from these areas that the members of the iinkundla of Nkaneng come (see p. 40).

12   Malema was the president of the ANC Youth League and was expelled when he started pushing for a radical economic program. His new political party, surprisingly, won 6% of the vote, catapulting it into national prominence. See Shivambu and Smith 2014.

13   Luke Sinwell and Siphiwe Mbatha (2016) at the University of Johannesburg Research Chair in Social Change unit have conducted extensive research into the birth and operation of strike committees in the Lonmin strike, including the committees formed during the earlier Impala strike and the later Amplats strike.

14   When questioned by the Farlam Commission, the police were unable to provide satisfactory and credible reasons as to why they had delayed for an hour to provide medical assistance to the first group of strikers who were shot at the scene of the massacre. The commission noted that since the police had prearranged four mortuary vans and ordered four thousand rounds of ammunition in preparation for the operation, they should have anticipated that medical assistance would be required and had medical personnel at the scene. The commission referred this matter to the director of public prosecution for further investigation in order to establish whether there was any criminal liability on the part of the police.

15   Based on Socialist Group internal documents.

16   See Mayekiso 1996 for "civics" in South Africa. See also Adler and Steinberg 2000.

17   Bank (2011, 61) refers to Clifton Crais's (2002) notion of the power of the "cultural politics of the encounters." Critical events and encounters may, "as much as longer-term processes of change," provoke "new forms of consciousness and political imagination in South Africa, and have challenged accepted ideas of progress and development."

18   This was reported to me by Rehad Desai, who was filming the congress. The heart-rending scenes will be released in a forthcoming documentary.

19   Reflecting on recent developments in the workers' struggle internationally, Ness and Azzellini (2011, 7) ask: "Does the escalating wave of workers' direct action from 2000 to 2010 foreshadow an impending, sustained shift towards labor insurgency and direct action rooted in working-class consciousness?"

Chapter 3: Makoko Slum Settlement

1   See, for example, Babalobi 2013; Marx, Stoker, and Suri 2013; Gunther 2012; Hahn 2010; Awofeso 2011; Buttenheim 2008; Werlin 2006; Weeks, Hill, Stow, Getis, and Fugate 2007; Pokhariyal 2005; Zulu, Dodoo, and Chika-Ezer 2002; and Aina 1989.

2   The Third Mainland Bridge is the longest in Nigeria (measuring over 7 miles in length) and the second-longest in Africa after the 6 October Bridge in Cairo (Atubi 2010; Tripa-

thi 2005). It is one of three bridges linking mainland Lagos to Lagos Island. Third Mainland Bridge was commissioned in 1990 and remains one of the busiest bridges in Nigeria (Akanni 2010; Atubi 2010).

3　About 85,000 people are estimated to live on the land section of Makoko (Collins 2015; Ibiwoye 2014; Agbola and Agunbiade [2007] 2009).

4　The NHRC is an agency of the Nigerian government tasked with the responsibility of protecting the rights of citizens. The NHRC has not really been active in this area, however; it is perceived as one of the many inactive parastatal organizations of the federal government of Nigeria.

5　The Egun (Ogu) are non-Yoruba but indigenous to Lagos state. The Egun population also extends into Benin.

6　Lagoon Makoko residents pollute the lagoon by discharging waste into the lagoon waters. This is a major environmental problem, which the state has not strategically addressed.

7　The "health facilities" referred to here are actually dispensaries run by quacks.

8　Environmental sanitation is a periodic cleaning exercise of the immediate environment of a household or neighborhood. It usually takes place on the last Saturday of the month. The practice was introduced in 1984 by the regime of General Muhammadu Buhari to stem the tide of environmental filth in many neighborhoods in Nigeria.

Chapter 4: The Ayotzinapa Massacre

Endnote: From the short story "Tenga para que se entretenga" (Pacheco's [1972] 1997).

1　"Normalistas" are students of the normal school system, which comprises 245 institutions. These schools provide training for primary school teachers in Mexico.

2　On October 2, 1968, the army and the Olympia Battalion, a special police squad, shot (in cold blood) and killed hundreds of students attending a demonstration in the Plaza of the Three Cultures in Tlatelolco, Mexico City. The clash between the Mexican student movement and the city police had gone on for months, echoing the urban political turmoil worldwide during 1968. The massacre was condemned as a crime of state. The motto "The state did it" (Fue el Estado), seen now in all the demonstrations for Ayotzinapa, is rooted here.

3　"*Vivos se los llevaron, vivos los queremos!*"

4　They are the only institutions offering higher education to indigenous and poor students. Among them, the Ayotzinapa School has a long tradition of Marxist-Leninist-oriented and combative politics.

5　In November 2015, the National Human Rights Commission (CNDH) publicly questioned the government's failure to fully comply with the observations and requests made to them in regard to the investigations (José Antonio Román, "En caso de Iguala, insuficiente respuesta de la PGR a observaciones de CNDH," *La Jornada*, November 9, 2015). The latest data on the clandestine graves reported 105 buried bodies found in Iguala (Sergio Ocampo Arista, "Suman 105 los cuerpos encontrados," *La Jornada*, November 9, 2015).

6　Actions included protests, vigils, international solidarity tours, and the use of social media to raise awareness and support the cause of justice for the forty-three missing.

7　A glimpse of this cityscape can be seen in the short documentary *Ayotzinapa—Ciudad de México* (Imprenta de Luz 2014).

8   *"Fuera Peña!"*

9   See Julie Schwietert Collazo, "Ayotzinapa +43 'anti-monument' erected without permission in Mexico City," *Latin Correspondent*, April 30, 2015.

10 See Gustavo Castillo García, "En nueve meses, la PGR ha detenido a 108 personas," *La Jornada*, June 26, 2015.

11 See Blanche Petrich and Emir Olivares, "Entrega GIEI 'Informe Ayotzinapa' a autoridades federales," *La Jornada*, September 6, 2015. Tlachinollan, an NGO based in Tlapa, Guerrero, has accompanied the parents and supported them throughout the investigation process. The report Tlachinollan (2015) published—focusing on human rights—is one of the most complete and reliable so far.

12 The remains of Alejandro Mora, one of the missing students, were found and identified by forensic experts in December 2014. Popular mobilizations continue upholding the number forty-three.

13 The lead activist during the search for clandestine graves around Iguala, Jiménez, was forty-five years old. See Nash Jenkins, "The Mexican Activist Who Led the Search for Missing Students Has Been Killed," *TIME*, August 10, 2015. The banners were the work of Scottish artist Jan Nimmo and were based on the ones the parents carried in the first demonstration back in 2014.

14 *". . . presentación con vida."*

15 Names taken from the banners. Some of the parents were not present that day: some live in the United States, travel for international solidarity tours, or participate in demonstrations and actions in Guerrero.

16 The motto "We are all Ayotzinapa" echoes the phrase "We are all Marcos," a common refrain during the 1990s movement in support of the Zapatista Army of National Liberation (EZLN).

17 "¡Ni perdón, ni olvido, castigo a los asesinos!"

"¡Urgente, urgente, que renuncie el presidente!"
"¡Ni con tanques, ni metrallas, Ayotzi no se calla! ¡Ni con tanques, ni metrallas, el pueblo no se calla! ¡Ni con tanques, ni metrallas, México no se calla!"
"¡Fuera Peña!"

18 For decades, since it was first published in 1984, *La Jornada* has maintained a critical left-oriented editorial line. Though it has some limitations now, it continues to be one of the few sources of information about social movements in Mexico.

19 Five months later, the Inter-American Commission on Human Rights would label Mexico "the most dangerous country for journalists in Latin America": one out of every three documented murders since 2010 was committed here. Data reported 150 journalists killed in the region—that is, one every fourteen hours. *La Jornada*, November 3, 2015.

20 In this section I am drawing on Subcomandante Marcos's famous description of Chiapas, the state where the EZLN started an indigenous armed insurgency and declared war on the Mexican state in 1994. The text, entitled *The Southeast in Two Winds: A Storm and a Prophecy*, depicts the harsh social conditions in Chiapas in the year NAFTA was enacted. At the time, and still today, Guerrero, Chiapas, and Oaxaca are the poorest states in Mexico.

21 According to CNN-México, the minister of the interior released the plan in October, without specifying the number of troops to be deployed or the strategies to be used.

22   According to González (2015), Cabañas was an ex-member of the Communist Youth Party, leader of the FECSM, and leader of the Party of the Poor (PDLP) in Guerrero. The PDLP was first a political organization and then became a guerrilla organization in the late 1960s. Genaro Vázquez was a communist militant and founding member of the Independent Peasant Central, also a representative organization in the history of the Mexican peasant movement.

23   "*Maestro Cabañas, el pueblo ya te extraña!*" This political slogan, shouted by the young normalistas during the demonstrations for Ayotzinapa in Mexico City, shows an important connection between two generations of rural political militancy: the one born in the second half of twentieth century and the latest, born in the present one.

24   Rivero replaced Figueroa, who was forced to resign after Aguas Blancas. Rivero—now affiliated with the Party of the Democratic Revolution—was state governor in 2011 and up to the time of the massacre of Ayotzinapa. He stepped down in October 2014.

25   Hernández follows these rounds of dispossession across three major periods: first, the 1970s, with the transformation of Guerrero into a migrant labor supplier for export-oriented agribusiness in northwestern Mexico. Then, the mid-1980s, which saw increasing drug production and the transformation of the region into a major pool for the North American transnational migrant labor market. And finally, the 1990s and the enactment of NAFTA.

26   There have been eleven major structural reforms. Labor, fiscal, finance, transparency, education, energy, and telecommunications reforms are among the most important ones. In tandem they are considered to be the broadest and greatest reform package in Mexico's contemporary history. On this topic see also Fuentes (2015).

27   The book includes a map showing the current operation of drug cartels in sixty-five municipalities. The major ones are United Warriors, The Reds, The Templar Knights, New Generation Jalisco Cartel, The Michoacana Family, Independent Cartel of Acapulco, The Squirrels, The Granados, and The Viagras. According to the author, some of these criminal organizations are linked to gold mines in the state and to exports of mineral ore to China (González 2015, 57–72).

28   González also provides information on some of the local responses that have emerged to counteract this violence, including at least five "revolutionary groups" active in the state: the PROCUP, EPR, ERPI, FARP, and FARP-LP. In addition, the work of Sierra (2015) documents the organization of self-defense community police in forty-six of the eighty-one municipalities.

29   The percentage of the migrants of Guerrero—together with those of Chiapas, Oaxaca, and Veracruz—traveling undocumented to the United States has risen from 68.5% in 1995 to 92.8% in 2005. About 13% of the population of Guerrero currently resides in the United States (González 2015, 40).

30   "*Al Zócalo!*"

Chapter 5: The Case of the West Zone

1   Rio de Janeiro is known worldwide for its mountains and hills—and the favelas that have consequently been installed above the city since the beginning of the twenty-first century. This geography has played a part in most of the city's conflicts, since it is a source of con-

stant challenge and poor living conditions for the favelas' inhabitants.

2   These are criminal groups in which various agents of the state (policemen, plumbers, and the military) take part—as well as drug traffickers—to economically exploit people living in certain areas of Rio de Janeiro, especially the West Zone. We will hear more on the milícias further on in this chapter.

3   The Brazilian equivalent of the Slutwalk, a movement that started in Canada, in 2011, by the allegation of a police officer that "women should avoid dressing like sluts" as a precaution against sexual assault, is a transnational movement of marches that gather feminists worldwide.

4   Sometimes referred to as the Battle of Seattle, the protests that took place in this city in 1999 became the benchmark of the antiglobalization movement, with an intense participation of young people and a never-before-seen coordination of repressive techniques by the US police.

5   UPP stands for Pacifying Police Unit, a Rio de Janeiro initiative started in 2008 that has been installed in more than forty favelas. The program has been praised for lowering homicide rates and paving the way for infrastructure and social programs to enter favelas, but criticized for ongoing police violence, human rights violations, lack of accompanying social projects, and ultimately failing in its promise to deliver peace to communities.

Chapter 6: The Uruguayan Recyclers' Union

1   The number of clasificadores is hotly debated, with the UCRUS citing the figure of 9,000 and the municipal government, basing itself on a recent representative sample, citing the lower figure of 3,188.

2   Padre Cacho was an Uruguayan priest inspired by liberation theology who lived in poor neighborhoods in order to "find Jesus among the poor." He became particularly associated with the cause of clasificadores. He is regarded as important in popularizing the term clasificador to replace *hurgador* (rummager), which was widely regarded as derogatory.

3   The power that garbage workers' strikes hold over municipal governments has long been recognized: from the Memphis Garbage Strike of 1968 (Collins 1988) and the refuse strike of the British Winter of Discontent of 1978–1979 (Martin López 2014) to the recent strike of Rio de Janeiro garbage workers timed to coincide with the World Cup.

4   Uruguay in turn is one of the few countries in the world to have every national trade union (one per sector) affiliated to a central national body. The federation had several unsuccessful predecessors, which splintered due to ideological differences (such as during the Cold War) or repression (during the 1973–1985 dictatorship). The federation in its current guise was founded after trade unions were legalized toward the end of the dictatorship. It held a victorious May Day rally in 1984 under the banner of "PIT-CNT: A Single Trade-Union Movement" (González Sierra 1989).

5   In some ways this can also be seen as a dispute between conflicting rights: the right of the clasificadores to work and circulate throughout the city versus animal rights and children's rights (some used a children's-rights-based discourse to criticize clasificadores who worked with their children and occasionally sent them inside containers to remove recyclables).

6   Uruguayan word meaning "leftovers." It is used by clasificadores to refer to the things

they take home from the waste stream for domestic consumption. It refers principally to food but can also refer to clothing, ornaments, and so on.

7   *El País* ran a story on the developing conflict on September 17, 2014.

8   See www.oxforddictionaries.com.

9   Unions affiliated to the FORU went somewhat further than the UCRUS in the militancy of their actions. In the 1922 municipal waste workers' strike, for example, strikers put bombs in bins to discourage strikebreakers from collecting them, leaving two dead as a result (Errandonea and Costabile 1968, 115).

10 Profound thanks go to the militants of the UCRUS, for allowing me to accompany them, and to my colleague Giorgio Baldelli, who not only provided invaluable company as he researched the UCRUS and clasificadores at the same time but also allowed me access to some interview material used in this chapter.

Chapter 7: The Nonadanga Eviction in Kolkata

1   Revised from an earlier piece, "Nonadanga Eviction: Questioning the Right to the City," *Economic and Political Weekly* 47 (17): 13–15.

2   A crore is ten million, so Rs 250,000 crore = Rs 2.5 trillion, or about US$75 billion in 1996.

Index

About Haymarket Books

Haymarket Books is a nonprofit, progressive book distributor and publisher, a project of the Center for Economic Research and Social Change. We believe that activists need to take ideas, history, and politics into the many struggles for social justice today. Learning the lessons of past victories, as well as defeats, can arm a new generation of fighters for a better world. As Karl Marx said, "The philosophers have merely interpreted the world; the point, however, is to change it."

We take inspiration and courage from our namesakes, the Haymarket Martyrs, who gave their lives fighting for a better world. Their 1886 struggle for the eight-hour day, which gave us May Day, the international workers' holiday, reminds workers around the world that ordinary people can organize and struggle for their own liberation. These struggles continue today across the globe—struggles against oppression, exploitation, hunger, and poverty.

It was August Spies, one of the Martyrs targeted for being an immigrant and an anarchist, who predicted the battles being fought to this day. "If you think that by hanging us you can stamp out the labor movement," Spies told the judge, "then hang us. Here you will tread upon a spark, but here, and there, and behind you, and in front of you, and everywhere, the flames will blaze up. It is a subterranean fire. You cannot put it out. The ground is on fire upon which you stand."

We could not succeed in our publishing efforts without the generous financial support of our readers. Many people contribute to our project through the Haymarket Sustainers program, where donors receive free books in return for their monetary support. If you would like to be a part of this program, please contact us at info@haymarketbooks.org.

Shop our full catalog online at www.haymarketbooks.org.

Also Available from Haymarket Books

African Struggles Today: Social Movements since Independence
Peter Dwyer and Leo Zeilig

Apartheid Israel: The Politics of an Analogy
Edited by Jon Soske and Sean Jacobs, Foreword by Achile Mbembe

BRICS: An Anti-Capitalist Critique
Edited and introduced by Patrick Bond and Ana Garcia

Building Global Labor Solidarity in a Time of Accelerating Globalization
Edited by Kim Scipes

China on Strike: Narratives of Workers' Resistance
Edited by Hao Ren, English edition edited by Zhongjin Li and Eli Friedman

Class Struggle and Resistance in Africa
Edited by Leo Zeilig

Freedom Is a Constant Struggle: Ferguson, Palestine, and the Foundations of a Movement
Angela Y. Davis

Europe in Revolt: Mapping the New European Left
Edited by Catarina Príncipe and Bhaskar Sunkara

The Last Day of Oppression and the First Day of the Same: The Politics and Economics of the New Latin American Left
Jeffery R. Webber

Lineages of Revolt: Issues of Contemporary Capitalism in the Middle East
Adam Hanieh

Red October: Left-Indigenous Struggles in Modern Bolivia
Jeffery R. Webber

Reproductive Rights and Wrongs: The Politics of Global Population Control
Betsy Hartmann